SAMURAI

ARMS · ARMOR · COSTUME

SAMURAI
ARMS · ARMOR · COSTUME

MITSUO KURE

CHARTWELL
BOOKS, INC.

This edition published in 2007 by

CHARTWELL BOOKS, INC.
A Division of
BOOK SALES, INC.
114 Northfield Avenue
Edison, New Jersey 08837

ISBN-13 978-0-7858-2208-0
ISBN-10 0-7858-2208-9

© 2007 Compendium Publishing, 43 Frith Street,
London W1D 4SA, UK

Cataloging-in-Publication data is available for the Library of
Congress

Printed and bound in China

Design:Cara Rogers/Compendium Design

Page 1: *Toseigusoku armor with deer helmet—see pp104–107.*

Page 2: *Lady's walking-out or traveling costume of the Kamakura period—see pp42–45.*

Right: *Lady's costume of the Edo period—see pp192–195.*

CONTENTS

PREFACE

After my first photographic book on samurai armor was published a few years ago, I received many letters from its readers. Even members of the costume design team for an American blockbuster movie were in contact with me. Keen readers will have noticed the similarity of the armor in my book and the armor designed for that movie, which I shall, alas, have to leave unnamed.

In the past, I had concentrated much more upon the armor itself and tended to neglect both the tunics worn under the armor and the samurai's everyday clothing. However, one day, while surfing the Internet, I came across a website specializing in Japanese historical costume. The site was that of a company supplying clothing and tools that were mainly for Buddhist temples, and whose manager was also a specialist in Japanese historical costume.

It was then that I realized how important it is to have armor and costume depicted as it was actually worn, i.e. over the appropriate kimono or tunic. As may have been evident to any expert reader of my first book, some of the photographed re-enactors shown there wore highly decorative armor over what were just simple, everyday kimonos. Historically, this is very unlikely to have been the case. Indeed, the undergarments of the high-class samurai were as rich as his armor. So, I decided to contact the curator of a private museum in Kyoto.

Actually, I had visited the museum previously and enjoyed seeing the exhibits, along with the small corner that had been made available for the taking of photographs. It consisted of a stage placed where once stood the prince's room some 700 years ago, and had been restored with mannequins playing the game of "Go." Tourists could dress in court costume, free of charge, and then take photographs.

So, for this new project, it was obvious that I needed the curator's help and cooperation, or all my intended efforts would be fruitless. Thus, I made another trip to Kyoto and visited his office. After I described to him my plan to create a new type of book of samurai costume, we went on to discuss the general problem of the historical costumes as used in the aforementioned movie. We agreed that some of the costumes used in it were quite inaccurate. Furthermore, the curator informed me that he too had always been annoyed by the general use in such films of inaccurate design and inappropriate materials that did not correspond to their supposed historical period. As a clothes and costume specialist, perhaps he expected too much of the movie's costume designer; whereas I always remain very critical of armor depicted in samurai movies.

In fact, a friend of mine, the historical novelist, Mr Togo, and I have always been disturbed by the general levels of inaccuracy of costumes in samurai movies. In some, a type of armor has been used for a storyline set in a completely different period. Even allowing for artistic freedom, such errors are sometimes simply not acceptable. Of course, movie directors will say that they do try their best, but that a movie is not a historical textbook. Nevertheless, such mistakes can easily be avoided by calling upon the services of a qualified historical adviser.

With this premise in mind, I have intended all along that this book will depict samurai costumes and armor as accurately as possible for each relevant era. The actual armor used for photography was borrowed from dedicated collectors and replica armor retail outlets. These sources were all willing to help me and I very much appreciate their collaboration.

Obviously, within the scope of a single book, I can neither show the reader all the costumes I wanted to include, nor reproduce all of the costumes described. However, by the fortunate associations and with the collaboration of the invaluable sources described above, I can say safely that I have included in the following pages the most important of all the samurai costumes. I have also been able to show some female costumes (and of their servants) of the samurai class and which are particularly beautiful and fascinating. Overall, I hope and expect that costume designers, as well as other readers, will be able to enjoy and benefit from the selection.

So, with the enormous help of all involved, especially that of the Japanese costume museum in Kyoto, I have been able to complete this book. In particular, I would also like to express my deepest gratitude to Ms Tatsuko Takagaki, who packed the precious costumes for dispatch to me for the photographic sessions.

In addition to costume, armor, and dress, I have also included some information of samurai hairstyles within the relevant descriptive texts. Throughout history, the samurai warrior knotted his hair. Today, it was not easy to find models with hair long enough to tie up in the traditional knot! So, in some cases I had to hire wigs from a specialist outlet. Alas, this being a relatively expensive exercise, I could not include all the hairstyles that I would have liked. Nevertheless, I trust that the reader will find this a valuable bonus to the rest of the text descriptions.

Lastly, I would like to thank my old friend and co-author of my first book, Ghislaine Gamaggio Kruit, for correcting my poor English and making it come alive in these pages.

MITSUO KURE
2006

INTRODUCTION

The Japanese word for traditional clothes is kimono, while western-style clothes are called yofuku. Although now widely used, the word kimono translates literally as "things to be worn". Based on this meaning, an account of the history of the kimono could stretch far into history - to the beginning of human clothing! On the other hand, when the Japanese speak of "kimono", they are commonly referring to the costume that appeared in the Edo period (1600 and later). In practice, therefore, the fuller history of Japanese costume dates from around that same period.

Another term that is often encountered in this context is kosode, the more pragmatic word for "traditional Japanese clothes"(even though, strictly speaking, this translates as "small sleeve"). Both these words, especially kosode, will appear often in any study of samurai costume history.

ENTER THE SAMURAI

Any attempt at pinpointing when the samurai appeared in Japanese history would be futile, since the date and manner of their arrival still remains one of the most important debates for modern historians. One could relate a string of facts and the many points of view and yet still not be able to give a satisfactory answer. The interested reader might refer to Mitsuo Kure's second book, Samurai: An Illustrated History, where the issue is discussed much more extensively than one can hope to do here. Its coverage of the subject should suffice for the time being, while research and discussions still continue.

In ancient times, the people whom we today refer to as samurai were more specifically categorized by names such as mononofu (man holding weapons), musha ("a man of the martial art") tsuwamono ("a strong man") or bushi ("a man of arms"), although this latter is more a Chinese than true Japanese term. Originally, the word samurai itself meant "a man who serves an aristocrat". But by the year 1000, at the latest, the samurai distinguished themselves as warriors and were regarded by Japanese society as its military specialists. It is now generally accepted that the term samurai in normal use means "warrior".

The islands of Japan stretch from the southwest to the northeast and have a monsoon climate. The southern part of Japan, including the city of Kyoto, is especially hot and humid in the summer. Japanese clothes developed in a way that suited the climate. The tunics, for example, were made of hemp and linen, and were light and airy. On the other hand, aristocrats wore expensive silk, which whilst also light, was used more because it was visually ostentatious and glamorous, a clear indication of their wealth and the fact that they could afford to wear garments of such costly material.

From the year 710, the Emperor's court was at Nara (near modern Kyoto). There is a view now generally accepted that "civilization" was brought to them by Chinese and Korean immigrants and other refugees. The court adopted the Chinese writing system, let Buddhism flow in, spread imported literature and applied their legal system. It is hardly surprising that the Emperor's court during the Asuka (a part of Nara, once a political center) and Nara period also copied the clothing style of the Chinese Tang dynasty.

However, when the Japanese capital was moved from Nara to Kyoto in the year 794, a distinctive Japanese culture started to blossom. The Japanese samurai dress style also started to take shape at this time. There was no official samurai class per se until the mid-Heian period (between 900 and 1100); but the first samurai as a type of warrior had indeed evolved. These were men hired by and integrated into the aristocrats' political system. Subsequently, they then wore the same upper-class clothes as their patrons.

EARLY CLOTHING

Generally, aristocratic clothing consisted of white underwear (shirokosode), shorts (ohguchi), trousers (uenohakama) and jacket (hitoe). The shorts had a belt sewn into the cloth, which was tied at the waist on the left side. The trousers were tied in the back and front, with two cloth belts emanating from the flaps of each trouser leg. Of these trousers, there were many variations in style. Over this outfit they wore a coat (hou). The coat's color was strictly dictated by the position of the aristocrat.

A lower-class samurai (see also pages 28-31) from the Kamakura period (1192-1333), the era in which the Mongol Empire in mainland Asia reached its height and attempted its first, but abortive, invasion of Japan in 1274 on Kyushu.

A light foot soldier of the kind called ashigaru, auxiliary combatants who emerged in the Muromachi period (see also pages 82-85). The ashigaru did not usually wear the hakama, but when such "trousers" were necessary, they were usually folded up into the lower part of the kososde or tucked into the obi belt in this way for ease of movement in battle.

Later, aristocrats started to wear what was called a hunting outfit (*kariginu*), which was originally the daily, informal dress of the common people.

In the Kamakura period (1192-1336), samurai formal dress was an ornate version of the kariginu. They had a round neck and comparatively large sleeves, sewn together only at the rear and was open at the armpit. A jacket called a *suikan* (meaning "washed with water and dried") was also worn by the common people and looked very similar to the kariginu, but it tied with two cords in the back of the neck. The suikan sleeves consisted of two tubes of fabric sewn onto each other and attached to the main body of cloth at the back. Each seam was reinforced by two chrysanthemum-shaped knots called *kikutoji*. The seams on the chest also had two kikutoji. These typical knots also appear on the so-termed hitatare costume, which became symbolic of the Heian period.

The hitatare of the Heian period (794-1185) were the working cloths of the commoner. They were adopted by the samurai and had already become their formal dress in the Kamakura period. Unlike the hou, the hitatare had a neck part similar to today's kimono. For men, the right part of the collar folded under the left, whereas for ladies it was the reverse. They also wore a trouser suit called *hakama* (a word for trousers that is in use even today). Later, the hitatare and hakama-style costume were merely referred to collectively as hitatare, because they were always worn together. The upper side of the hakama had an oblong, triangular slit on both sides. This divided the trousers into two sections of front and back. There were belts hanging from both the front and the back flap. The front belt was tied to the rear and rear to the front. This was very different from the *ohguchi*, which tied at the left side.

In terms of practicality, the question might well arise as to how they dealt with nature's call, when caught up in the hectic tumult of the battlefield! After all, the costumes were not exactly easy to undo and re-tie. The answer is difficult to come by, however, as costume books fail to clarify this mundane issue. So readers are left to their own creative conjectures.

However, to continue the descriptions: the sleeve on the hitatare jacket tied at the wrist with a cord so that it wouldn't hinder the wearer while working or fighting. The hakama trousers had cords at the bottom for the same reason and they were tied under the knee when the leg protectors were worn. The excess cloth of the hakama legs folded over the knot, thereby hiding it. The cord was usually white; but if not, it would have been of a color different from that of the cloth, as this color contrast was considered more ornamental.

The tunics of the upper-class samurai were made from silk and in the later Muromachi period were often emblazoned with an ostentatious, large family crest. Because of this embellishment or similarly representative marking on the outfit, this type of hitatare was called *daimon* meaning "big crest".

A study of the development of the outfits makes it clear that commoners' clothes were adopted sooner or later by the upper class. Later, these also became the formal dress of the samurai and aristocrats. There is a simple reason for this in that they were far more comfortable and functional.

EARLY FEMALE COSTUME

Women's' clothes in the Heian period were basically the same as that of the men, namely a shirt and trousers. The difference was that women wore more colorful clothes, even though the material was essentially the same. However, they might have also carried or worn some accessories, such as a cloth bag, a dagger, an amulet or a Buddhist letter in Sanskrit for good fortune and protection. Women's hairstyles were different, of course.

The *kosode* shirt was long enough to reach the floor and had relatively small sleeve holes. On top of the kosode, aristocrats, samurai wives and rich women wore a jacket called an *uchikake*. The ladies of the court wore layer upon layer of upper garments, such as those called the *hitoe*, *uchigi* and *kinu*.

These were actually Chinese-based clothes in origin, and when twelve layers had been reached, the outfit was called *junihitoe*, or "twelve layers-in-one". The hakama trousers for ladies had the same cut as the men's, but were often longer. Often, in order to keep the attire simple, the hakama was not worn by women when at home or even for walking outdoors. Later, the kosode was tied with a belt (*obi*). The outfit became more refined over time and evolved into a standard item of clothing, i.e. the female Japanese kimono that we know today.

SAMURAI CLOTHING

As one might imagine, the excess of baggy fabric in the hitatare costume worn under the *oyoroi*-style armor might actually have been quite a nuisance. Indeed, as fighting techniques changed, such costumes had to be adapted for greater practicality

In the late Heian and early Kamakura periods, samurai fought while wearing elaborate and ornamental costumes. At that time, this did not hinder them unduly, as they were mostly horse-riding archers and their battles were relatively small in scale, with only a few hundred deployed on foot in the battlefield.

Being horse riders and masters, the samurai often relied upon personal foot soldiers called *ashigaru* ("light-footed soldiers"), whose presence was first recognized in the late-Heian period and their role, undertaken by lower-class samurai, became more evident in the late-Muromachi period, when they also received this specific name. These foot soldiers wore less elaborate armor and were more mobile than their horse-riding masters. Fighting alongside the samurai, such foot soldiers were not usually thought of by them as being full fighting men and so were never classified as samurai. Further, whilst they were responsible for certain battlefield tasks, they had only a limited role in battle tactics.

However, historians have shown that the importance of the ashigaru as attendants in battle cannot be neglected. Indeed, their presence in a conflict goes some way into explaining why their samurai masters were able to come to battle dressed in impractical and cumbersome costumes. In reality, the real ground fighting was done by the ashigaru foot soldiers.

As wars intensified and battles became larger, the samurai found that they too were increasingly obliged to fight on foot. Conflicts often became little more than siege warfare, with the fighting taking place around castles. Consequently, attacking a well-defended fortress required an approach on foot.

Furthermore, the number of soldiers in action increased. With so many men now fighting, the old-style hitatare outfit became inconvenient, even though it had been adopted from working clothes for their inherent functional mobility. Quite simply, the baggy sleeves got in the way; and in an emergency, a samurai would often tear off his sleeves to make battle easier. Alternatively, or if he was less ruthless, he might tie up the sleeves with cords so as to facilitate movement. Thus, simple necessity changed the hitatare style to one with narrower sleeves and called *yoroi-hitatare* ("under-armor hitatare").

At that time, all fabric was typically woven to a measured size of approximately 7½ inches by 330 ft (35 cm x 10 m) and was rolled onto a wooden board. Patterns for clothes were adapted to the fabric's width, so as not to waste any material. For example, the sleeve of the hitatare was sewn from a one-and-a-half width piece of cloth. The back piece of the body part consisted of two pieces of a single roll-width, and the front of two pieces of half-a-roll. The panels were sewn with a loose stitch, while seams were reinforced with kikutoji ornate knots. When the material became stained or worn, the section was easily replaced with new fabric.

Theoretically, therefore, the samurai never wore patched clothes, just like the aristocrat class. However, in practice, the samurai were not usually rich enough to keep replacing clothing panels and so they simplified the costumes in order to facilitate repairs. Only the upper sides of sleeves were sewn directly onto the body section, so that the underarm area was not only open for ventilation, but also so that the sleeve was easily exchanged when soiled. Kikutoji too were later down-graded to a simpler type of knot that was made form cord.

As already mentioned, the costumes bore the big daimon family crests. There were usually five of them: two on the upper chest, two on the front of the sleeve and one on the upper back. The side of the hitatare was not sewn and was open (similar to a hou). The fronts of both sleeves were not stitched to the body panels, but fastened only on the back at the shoulder.

As opposed to Western styles, traditional Japanese clothing was not made to "envelop" the body, but rather to "hang" over and around it. Thus, the suoh jacket, a type of hitatare, had a similar construction to that just described, with each of the front panels hung from the shoulders. It was fixed at the waist with a leather belt, so that the earlier use of a cord at the wrist, used to gather in the sleeve, was eliminated.

By the Muromachi period (1336-1392), samurai usually wore the suoh with hakama long trousers, though shorter hakama called *ko-suoh* were not uncommon. Lower class samurai often wore even shorter hakama called *yonobakama* while the ashigaru of later times wore close-fitting trousers called *momohiki*.

In the late Muromachi period, during the Sengoku era (1482-1558) and that is known as the "Age of the Country at War," the hitatare and the suoh jackets became to be regarded as formal dress. In daily life, the samurai wore jackets called *kataginu*. These were basically a hitatare without sleeves. Later, the kataginu also became formal dress.

Seen from the rear, with his bow quiver and turnip-shaped arrowhead, a samurai archer of the Muromachi-Sengoku period in typical kawazutsumi armor, with its extensive rear protection (see also pages 96-99).

LATER FEMALE COSTUME

As the Kamakura era evolved into the Muromachi period, comings and goings greatly increased between Kyoto and the towns of Kamakura and Edo in the Kanto area (Tokyo as it is known today), So, it was not uncommon to see even women traveling alone along the main road. When traveling in this way, women would wear a cape-like jacket called a *utigi* on top of a *hitoe* (a type of kimono jacket) and tie a wide obi belt at armpit height of. The utigi jacket was often slipped over the head in a style called katzugi or *kazuki* (meaning "put on over the head"). While traveling, women might slip their arms into the deep, hanging sleeves for comfort or warmth.

In the Muromachi period (1336-1392), female costume was simplified and the kosode jacket merely worn with a narrow obi belt. The sleeves of the kosode was generally shorter, but with a rounded shape. Even on formal occasions, slipping an uchikake over-garment on top the kosode would suffice. In summer, the uchikake was tied at the waist for convenience, as the protective warmth of the length was no longer required. On the other hand, the uchikake was often used as a blanket in winter.

CHANGES IN ARMOR AND DRESS

During the Sengoku period, the "Age of the Country at War", greater body coverage was required of the armor and more armor had to be made. This meant that there was insufficient time to create decorative costume and much less space where the armor could be visually embellished. Traditionally, the samurai had regarded their battle dress, as a costume honoring death, a beautiful shroud of sorts. So, the showier it was, the better it was regarded. As a result, the practicality of the new, full-body armor effectively ruled that previous form of decoration.

A jacket called a *doubuku* emerged in the Muromachi period and developed into the *haori,* (meaning "to put over"). It was first introduced as a quick, slip-on item used to protect the wearer and his armor in wet or cold weather on the battlefield. The early versions had sleeves, but these were removed in the Sengoku period so that the soldiers could use their arms more easily. A type of haori worn mainly on the battlefield had the special name of the *jinbaori*. It was a flamboyant garment when compared to the basic under-armor tunic. The jinbaori often had a long slit in the back creating two long flaps that lay over the sides of the horse while riding. Also, it provided easier access to the warrior's sword. The jinbaori jacket was often embroidered with an ornamental design, not unlike the surcoats of European medieval knights.

In the Edo period (from 1603) the samurai no longer fought in battle, so that the haori once again recovered its sleeves. So, ultimately, this ensured the jacket functioned much more in the way that had originally been intended: to protect its wearer against inclement weather.

The Edo period was characterized by being a stable, feudal society. The samurai became bureaucrats who did not need to distinguish themselves in order to gain high status and income. Subsequently, the haori they wore also became less flamboyant and evolved into a simple black coat, with the family crest or a small emblem painted or sewn on the sleeves and shoulder. As in any bureaucracy, there was no necessity to over-stress the individual's identity.

Interestingly, ironically perhaps, it was the haori of the common people that became more colorful and showy. This can be taken as a sign that the important roles in society were no longer being played by the samurai, but by the merchants, traders, artisans and farmers. By then they were the ones wishing to appear distinguished.

Geishas too began to wear the haori. Indeed, the geisha habit of wearing a haori on top of a kimono became popular amongst women in general in Edo period and has become standard dress female dress of today.

THE SAMURAI LEGACY

During periods of peace, formal costumes were once again worn at longer lengths. Thus, in the Edo period vassals and retainers at the shogun's court wore their clothes as long as they could.

(Historically, *shogun* was a social title and military rank equivalent to "general" or the highest officer in an army. At first, the Imperial court in Kyoto awarded this title first to the leaders of military expeditions, then later to the heads of military governments.)

The hem of the hakama was sometimes so outrageously long that it would drag along the wooden floors of Edo castle corridors with the wearer shuffling along on the inside of the trouser leg. Sleeves too became unfeasibly long.

The rules for weapon carrying also changed. For example, in Edojo Castle, the great fortress in Tokyo, the vassals' waiting

A samurai in the Chinese-inspired kartasane plate armor of the late Sengouku-Edo period, complete with two swords, a lance-type spear and an identifying, rear-worn banner (see also pages 150-153).

A Kyoto "special duty", anti-terrorist police officer of the late Edo period (see also pages 196-199) with tachi sword, dagger tucked into his obi belt and the famous "ten hands" jutte truncheon.

room was a place where it was prohibited to wear swords, although short daggers were still allowed. This was to curb the eventuality of dangerous fighting. On the other hand, the tunics were so long that these alone would have made any physical conflict most impractical.

Thus, the ferocious and brave samurai of almost legendary fame came to no longer exist and only the "tamed" ones remained. Even conflicts that did occur in the Edo period were mere reminders of a glorious past. For instance, the famed assassination by forty-seven samurai of the warlord against whom they had a strong grudge was an episode that provided the opportunity to prove that the samurai had, at least, once been warriors. Nevertheless, terrorism and counter-terrorism in the last flickerings of samurai history were as bloody as was their emergence in the Heian period.

Edo, known as Tokyo today, has been documented as having the largest population of any other city in the world at that time. In the city, there were two magistrates (*bugyo*). They were executive offices and had legal powers as well as simple police duties. One office controlled the south of the city, the other the north. They were independent from each other. Each employed his own inspectors and informers. The two principal positions in the system were chief inspector (*yoriki*) and inspector (*doshin*). Japanese TV programs and movies tend to show the yoriki and doshin as typical Edo guardsmen and liken them to samurai. They are tainted slightly by that legendary association.

The policemen wore very similar outfits to normal citizens, but they carried two swords and the very typical *jutte* (translated as "ten-hands"), a special hand tool used to arrest criminals and suspects. The doshin patrolled the city wearing a kosode and a haori like the town people, and it was only their two swords that differentiated them. He was not only recognizable to citizens because of the weapons, but also by a distinctively tied hair-knot.

For the average Edo citizen, this was the closest they got to encountering a samurai in daily life. Actually, the hierarchical position of these policemen was the lowest in the samurai class and they ranked more among the ashigaru foot soldiers; but Edo citizens addressed them as *osamurai-san* as a mark of respect.

At the police station it was usually the yoriki who interviewed and investigated suspects that were caught by the doshin. The doshin also did some investigating themselves at police boxes outside. The most basic, formal dress of the middle-class samurai

in Edo period was the *kamishishimo*, which means "top and bottom" and consists of a sleeveless kataginu jacket worn over a shirt-like kosode jacket and hakama trousers. Later the kataginu was replaced by the haori, also at formal occasions. The retainers of the warlord living in Edo wore similar clothes: a kosode and hakama with a haori as outdoor wear when walking outside. When on duty they were expected to wear a kataginu instead of the haori. This style remained constant throughout the Edo period until the Meiji imperial restoration.

THE DEMISE OF TRADITIONAL DRESS

When the Meiji Emperor and his supporters resumed power from the shogun, they decided to "modernize" Japan and adopt the contemporary international outlook and ethos necessary in order to counter or rather, perhaps, accommodate European and American colonialism. Indeed, the Meiji government was actually keen to introduce much Western culture into the country, in these efforts to modernize. So, once again the style of clothes changed, subject to influences from beyond Japan. Very quickly, traditional Japanese kimono culture was eroded by the acceptance of European clothes and styles. In fact, such dress was considered to be much more functional for everyday wear and work, a result of which has been that all forms of Japanese costume have been gradually replaced by western clothes in daily life.

Nowadays, the famous kimono, in all its traditional glory and with all its paraphernalia, is mostly only worn at very special occasions, such as weddings. Dressing in a kimono requires both considerable time (and often someone's help) as well as money, for they can be very expensive. In fact, the majority of modern Japanese people will probably never wear a kimono more than once or twice in a lifetime; and even then, women wear them more than men. Nevertheless, it is curious that most Japanese still agree that it is regrettable how kimono culture is so little appreciated in modern Japan.

In fact, the most obvious, maybe the only, survivor of the kimono culture is the ubiquitous yukata. This is a cotton bathrobe worn at public baths, in hotels and homes, and during street festivals. It much resembles the traditional kimono in shape and is often naively called a "kimono" by non-Japanese.

It is ironical, therefore, that what might be seen as Japan's first and final garment is the shroud in which the dead are now dressed.

HITATARE AND HABAKI
Late Heian to early Kamakura period

There were only two styles of early Japanese costume. One was of a jacket-like construction and the other we a longer coat with an unsewn flank. The *hitatare* is of the latter style, as are the *daimon* and *suoh* (which are described later). Here is a samurai leader wearing a hitatare with the *kikutoji* chrysanthemum-shaped seam reinforcement and sleeves that are tied with cord. Both side of the hitatare are unsewn, so that the chest consists of two long flaps hanging from the shoulder.

He also sports an *eboshi* hat or cap as headgear.

When untied, the long hakama trousers have side slits but could also be tied just below the knee with the lower legs covered by *habaki* leggings.

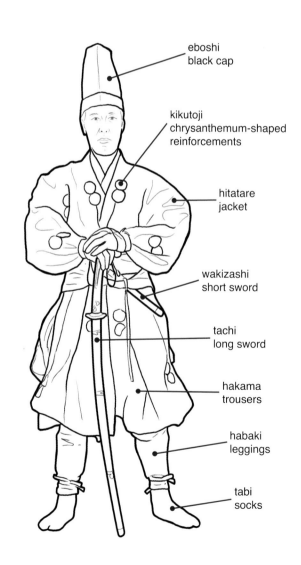

eboshi
black cap

kikutoji
chrysanthemum-shaped
reinforcements

hitatare
jacket

wakizashi
short sword

tachi
long sword

hakama
trousers

habaki
leggings

tabi
socks

Left and below: *The tachi sword is prominently on display in left and right side views, with the long, brightly-colored hakama trousers untied. The head band of the eboshi cap can be seen hanging at the rear.*

Above and left: *Front and partial side view of the hakama when tied up, showing the habaki leggings and the striking blue and white patterened leather socks.*

OHYOROI ARMOR
Late Heian to mid-Kamakura period

This is a samurai commander wearing a hitatare and a body protector on his right, independent of the main body armor. As here, the left sleeve of the hitatare was sometimes removed and folded into the waist belt in order to wear a protective gauntlet. This style was called *ko-gusoku* or "light armor"(see page 27). The donning of clothes and armor was always carried out starting from the left-hand side, e.g. first, the left leg protector, followed by the right side protector, then the left arm guard, and so on.

One exception was a pair of gloves that were put on from the right, as samurai of this era were basically archers. Consequently, when he needed to use his bow in battle, the samurai archer had to face his enemy from his left and protect his left side as a priority.

He is also wearing a pair of somewhat oversized bearskin shoes. As he usually fought on horseback, he avoided wearing waraji sandals that were the samurai footwear of later periods. Beneath the

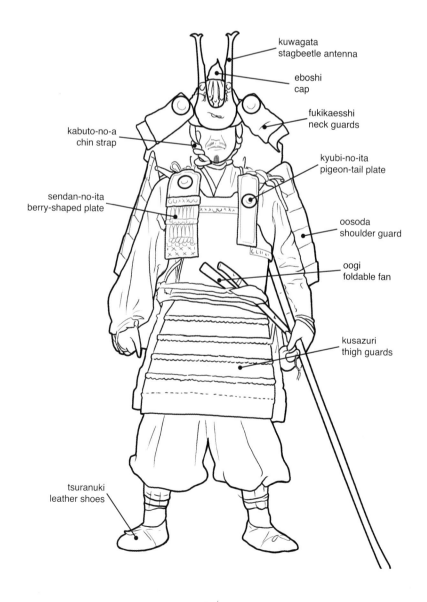

kuwagata
stagbeetle antenna

eboshi
cap

fukikaesshi
neck guards

kyubi-no-ita
pigeon-tail plate

kabuto-no-a
chin strap

sendan-no-ita
berry-shaped plate

oosoda
shoulder guard

oogi
foldable fan

kusazuri
thigh guards

tsuranuki
leather shoes

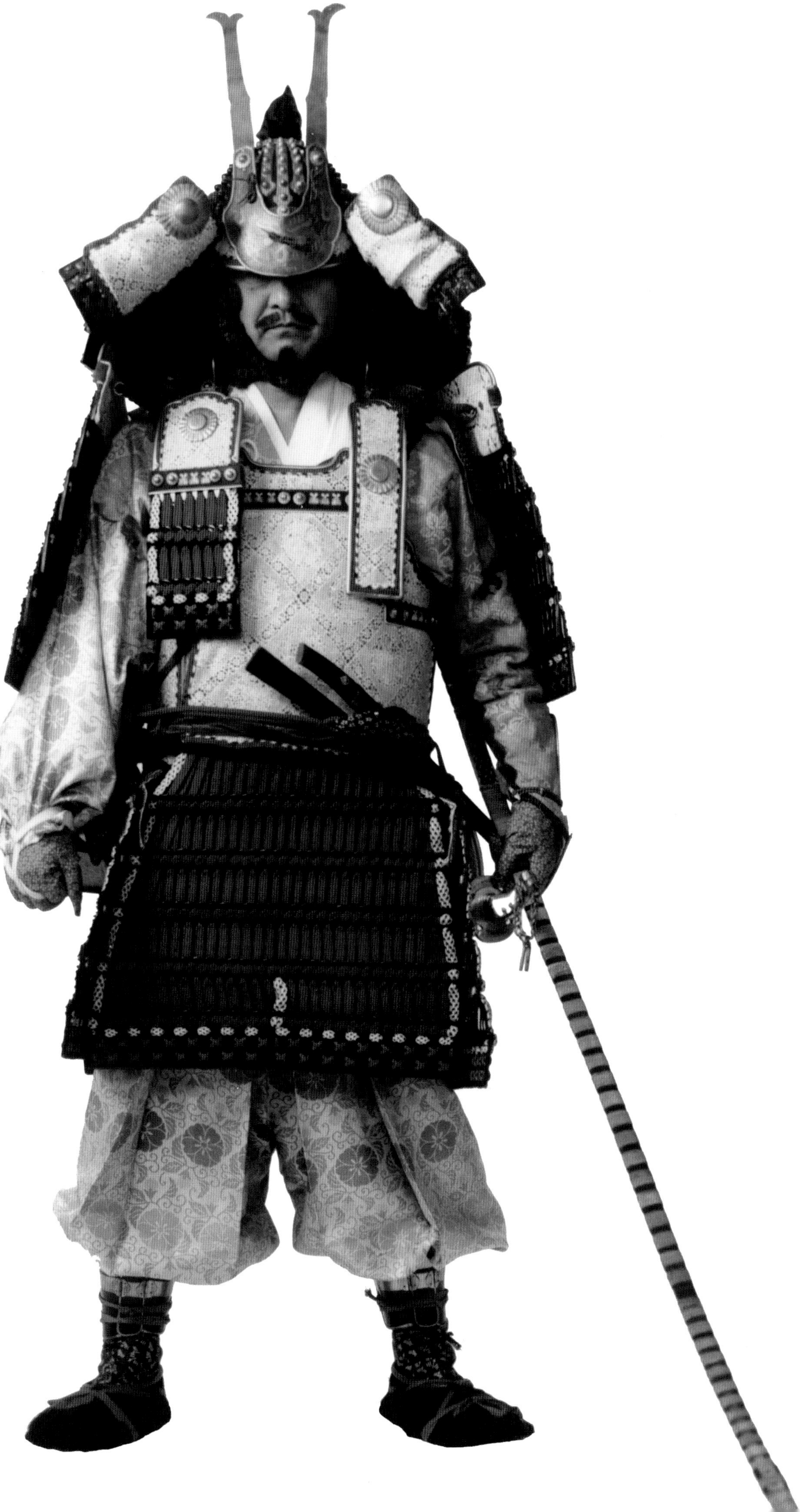

helmet, he wears an eboshi hat that is somewhat smaller and thinner in style from that worn by the warrior previously illustrated.

The thigh protector or *kusazuri* hanging from the breastplate, seems very long and almost reaches his knee, a style that is one of the distinctive features of the Ohyoroi period armor. (In contrast, recent TV programs and movies have shown samurai actors wearing very short armor, but perhaps for increased ease of movement and better maneuverability than actual inaccuracy). By the early Kamakura period, there was little choice about this style. Quite simply, it had to be worn long.

When riding, the warrior's saddle supported the bottom of the cuirass and eased the load on his shoulder, on which also hung heavy hangs. In addition, another factor that affected this style was that the physical stature of the Japanese people has changed over the centuries, now having longer legs than those of the old samurai.

Samurai of the late Kamakura period also wore armor of the ohyoroi style, but the kusazuri became shorter for fighting on foot. He carries quiver on his left, as he drew arrows downwards from the *ebira* (quiver), unlike western archers of the time.

When wearing a helmet, the *motodori* tied hair-knot or protrudes from the top. The knot also helped to keep the helmet secure on the head since there was no inner fastening device. The hat also functioned as buffer for the helmet, which has a sizeable hole as can bee seen in the photograph (right) although helmet bolts later became much smaller.

The bow is held with its string uppermost (although no actual bowstring has been attached in this particular pose).

At the rear, ohyoroi armor had cords hanging on the warrior's back were used to ensure that the *sode*

shoulder guard did not slip down when bending forwards to take a drink of water after a battle.

His *tachi* sword is rather straight in shape compared to later versions and hangs on the left with its blade is facing downward. The hilt is curved, making it easier to draw from the scabbard.

(There is a school of thought which postulates that the once-straight samurai sword acquired the characteristic curve as, in that shape, it was then easier to cut down the enemy when both adversaries were on horseback. If this theory were correct, then would not all of the world's traditional horse soldiers have used curved swords? Historical reality does not back this up, alas. In Europe, for example, the Roman cavalry employed a straight sword like its infantry's gladus, as did the many of the Germanic tribes with whom the Romans came into conflict towards the end of their Empire. Later, in the Crusades, even the Saracens used a straight sword at first, before adopting the curved scimitar.

The helmet's cheek guards proved to be rather awkward and hindered free use of the sword. Consequently, blows with the weapon tended to be horizontal at highest and generally in more of downwards direction, such a blow being incapable of inflicting a fatal wound to the enemy.

A right-hand side view of the archer showing the protective armor, bow, and arrows. The large sode acted as a shield, covering the archer's body as he turned to fire an arrow.

Left: *Rear of the ohyoroi armor, showing the hanging cords of the shoulder guards.*

Below: *Detail of the front of the helmet with its head and cheek guards.*

Above: *The armor as worn without the helmet, but still with the kusazuri thigh guard hanging from the breastplate.*

LOWER-CLASS SAMURAI
Kamakura period

The *hara-ate* style armor depicted here was worn over the hitatare, along with a cap similar to an eboshi, but folded down and with a strap. He carries a *nagamaki*, a form of lance or poled long-hilted) sword, but an alternative weapon might well have been the *naginata*, which differed in having a wider blade and which was also developed for use as a pike.

Generally, this class of samurai went barefoot when attending his master, although here he is also shown wearing a pair of sock-like garments called *tabi*. The sleeves had cords for tying them up, so as not to be in the way when in battle.

Note here that some researchers have a theory that the samurai's hitatare cord was hidden inside the garment with only its end hanging outside. Since the samurai's hitatare had a cloth lining, this might well have been possible. However, an authenticated genuine, antique samurai hitatare exists that has its cord fully outside the sleeve. So, while there are still a number of theories about the rather controversial sleeve cord, no fully satisfactory explanation has yet emerged.

Samurai of this period who carried any one of the poled-blade or lance-type weapons tended to avoid also wearing or employing the tachi long sword, as it limited maneuverability of the poled weapons other than the thrusting, long-bladed *yari*.

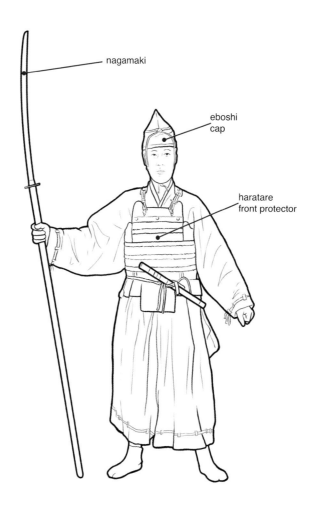

nagamaki

eboshi cap

haratare front protector

Above: *A closer look at the hara-ate style armor worn over the hitatare in this period.*

Left and right: *The the samurai ready for action, with his feet bare, his trousers tied up, and his nagamaki held at its point of balance. It was in the Kamakura period that the Mongol Empire reached its greatest extent in mainland Asia (by 1259) and set its sights on Japan. Its several threatening messages were ignored by the Kamakura and so the result was the first Mongol invasion attempt in 1274 on the island of Kyushu. After only a few hours of fighting, however, the large naval invasion fleet was forced to pull back because of adverse weather conditions.*

DOMARU ARMOR
Kamakura to Muromachi period

The hitatare is worn here with an ori-eboshi, a folded-down eboshi cap, a pair of blue and red kikutoji and left arm guard. At their lower rear, the hakama was tied below the knee but above the leggings.

As an archer, he would generally have worn an arm guard only on his left side but does wear a *kote* front and rear. Furthermore, in order to counter any surprise attack by an advanced guard, archers always advanced with an arrow ready strung in the bow, which was carried in the left hand.

Although the *utsubo* type of quiver was not particularly convenient for rapid shooting, it served well in protecting arrows from rain, which was another of any archer's enemies. Bowstrings became slack in the rain, so a spare was always carried on the left hip or attached to the scabbard.

If not an archer, he might have carried a naginata, as shown here, probably without wearing a sword .

Ohyoroi armor has a sizeable back guard, while the doumaru style had a shoulder guard in the form of a smaller plate hung on a shoulder strap. The thigh protector was constructed in seven pieces, with three at front and four on back, while ohyoroi had four, at the front, rear and both sides.

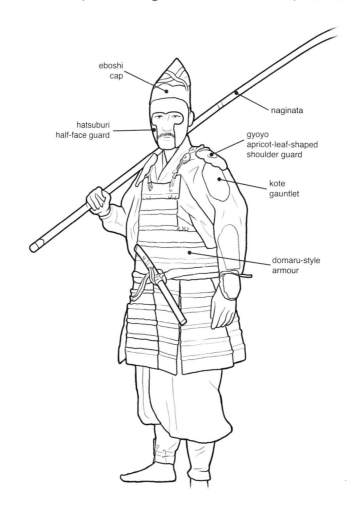

eboshi cap

naginata

hatsuburi half-face guard

gyoyo apricot-leaf-shaped shoulder guard

kote gauntlet

domaru-style armour

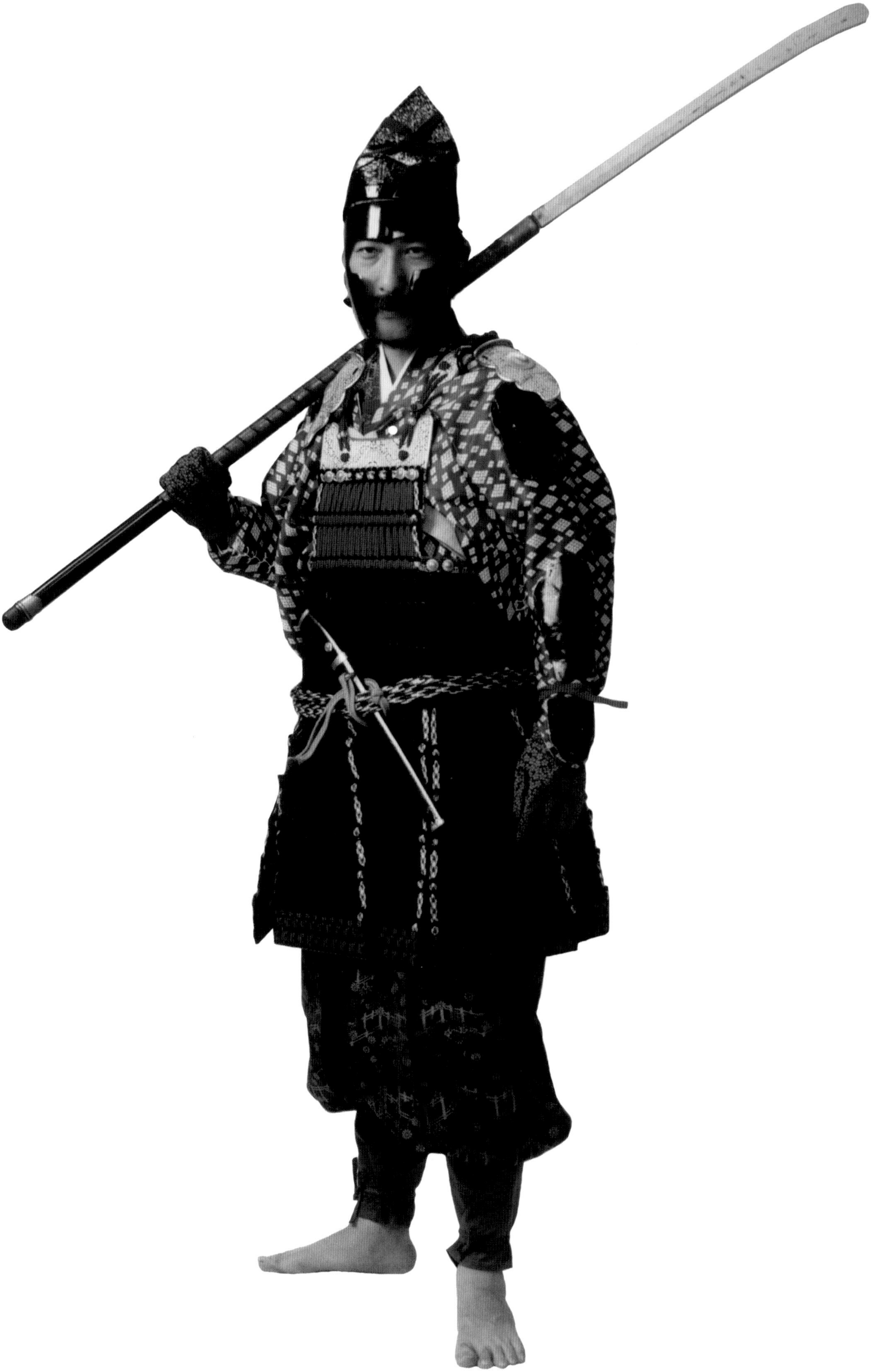

Right and below: When fighting as an archer, an arrow would be always ready and then the warrior would advance with the arrow already strung in the bow ready for action when advancing into any suspected ambush.

Above and left: *Rear and front view showing the extensive back and front thigh guards. The gauntlets worn here would have had only a couple or so protective metal plates sewn into them, a construction which preceded the introduction of chain mail.*

Without the armor and armed only with the short form of sword in its scabbard.

Above and right: *Without armor or naginata, showing suspension of the sword's scabbard from the white obi belt.*

Left: *As an archer, with the left sleeve removed at the shoulder and folded down into his waist belt, whilst on his right, his sleeve strap remains secured to his middle finger.*

DOMARU ARMOR WITH SHOULDER GUARD
Kamakura to Muromachi period

In its early forms, domaru armor had a small *gyoyo* (apricot-leaf) shoulder guard that evolved gradually in shape and was later incorporated into a much larger guard that was fully integrated into ohyoroi armor.

The samurai shown here is wearing doumaru armor that has both the large shoulder guard and gyoyo; but the position of the latter has now moved from upper shoulder to near the clavicle.

He has the usual samurai eboshi cap and waraji straw sandals on his feet.

The cord fastening device of the shoulder guard is similar in style to that of ohyoroi armor.

The tachi sword was attached to the waist belt with its curve uppermost, as evident in the side view.

In fact, the sword was regarded as defensive weapon or side arm in the battle, but as a foot soldier, his main weapon was the naginata poled blade.

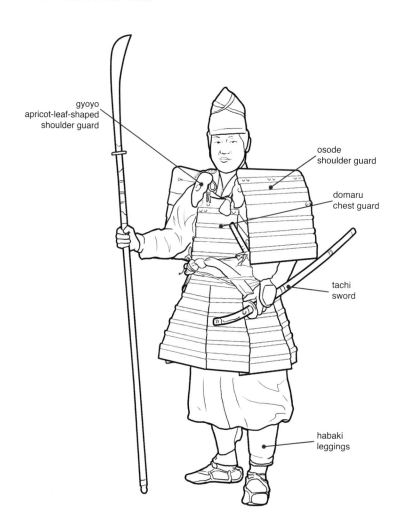

gyoyo
apricot-leaf-shaped
shoulder guard

osode
shoulder guard

domaru
chest guard

tachi
sword

habaki
leggings

Below: *Rear view showing the cord fastenings of the shoulder guard.*

Above: *Left side showing shoulder guard and sword in its traditional horizontal position. The large sode, that was once a part of ohyori armor was integrated into domaru armor, as it's lighter construction and greater protective maneuverabilty.*

Left and below: *On active duty and in the act of stopping and checking a woman at a roadblock, the samurai suddenly realizes that he has been inadvertently impolite and rude to a lady of high social rank and position. In making recompense, he bends down, but in such a way that both knees are not touching the ground This sitting style, called sonkyo, can be seen in sumo wrestling even today.*

LADY'S WALKING-OUT OR TRAVELING COSTUME
Kamakura period

This samurai lady is wearing a blue *uchiki* coat on top of a violet hitoe. In being fastened on her upper chest, the obi belt differs from that of later periods. Across her front, she also wears an amulet hanging from her left shoulder.

Most striking however, is her large hat and hemp fiber veil. The latter was worn as both front and rear protection from bright sunlight, insects and the commoner's gaze.

Of course, in order to see clearly, she needed to open the veil, as depicted over the page

Ladies of high social position would often to paint their faces white, white skin being regarded as one of the required attributes of a beautiful woman, especially if an aristocrat. The practice was not universal, except for ladies in the Emperor's court; but even a male samurai would lighten his face color if meeting the Emperor.

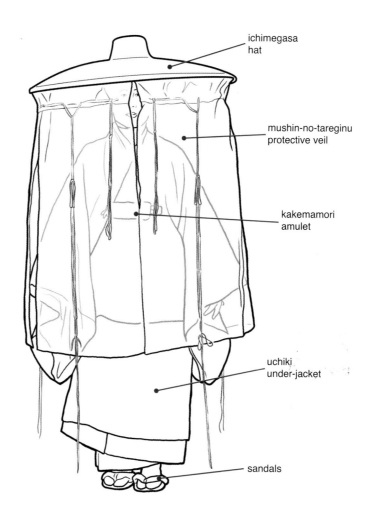

ichimegasa
hat

mushin-no-tareginu
protective veil

kakemamori
amulet

uchiki
under-jacket

sandals

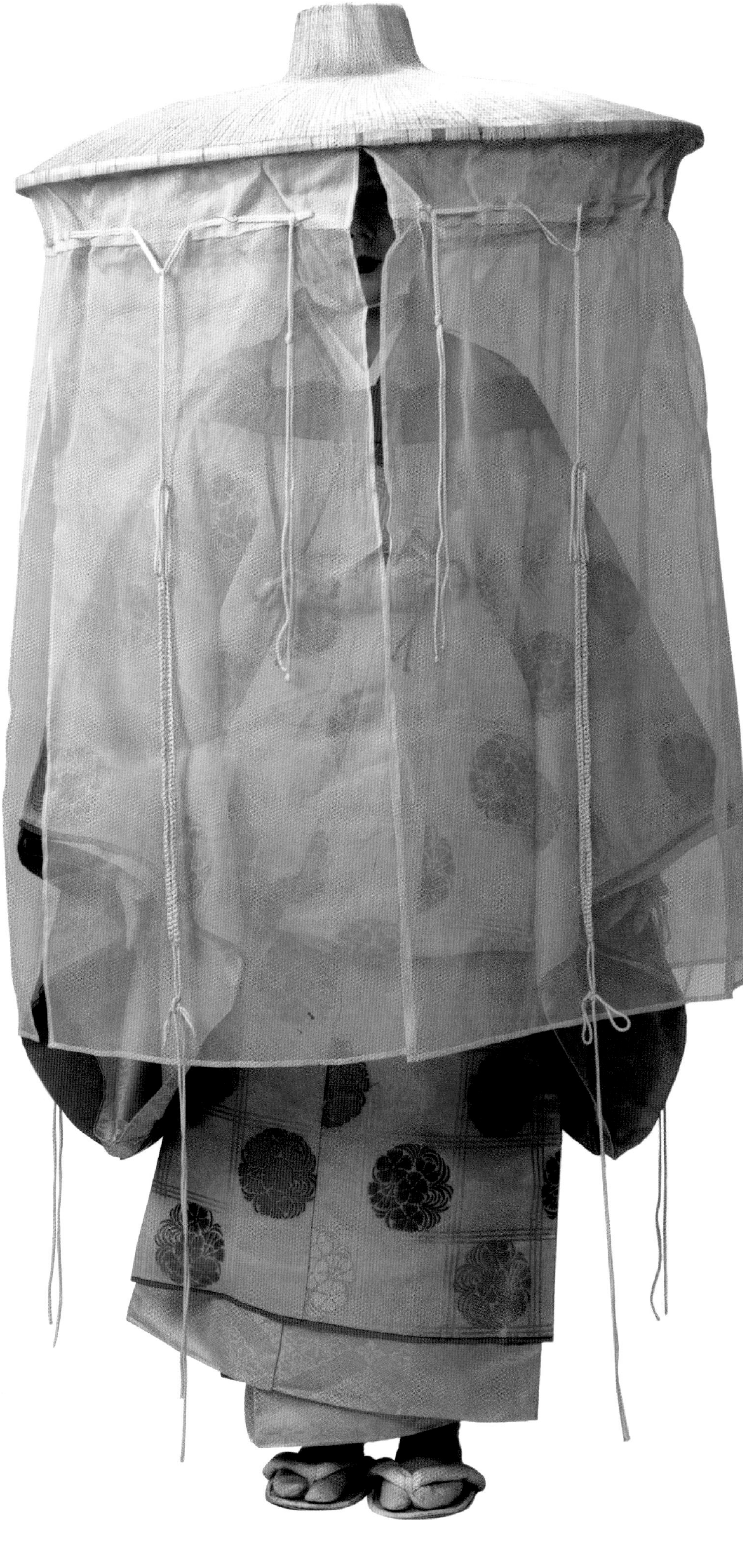

Right: Opening the veil in order to see and communicate more easily reveals the amulet worn across the front

Below: Rear view of the veil showing the symmetry of its overall design, front and rear.

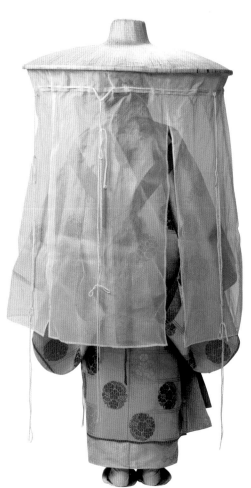

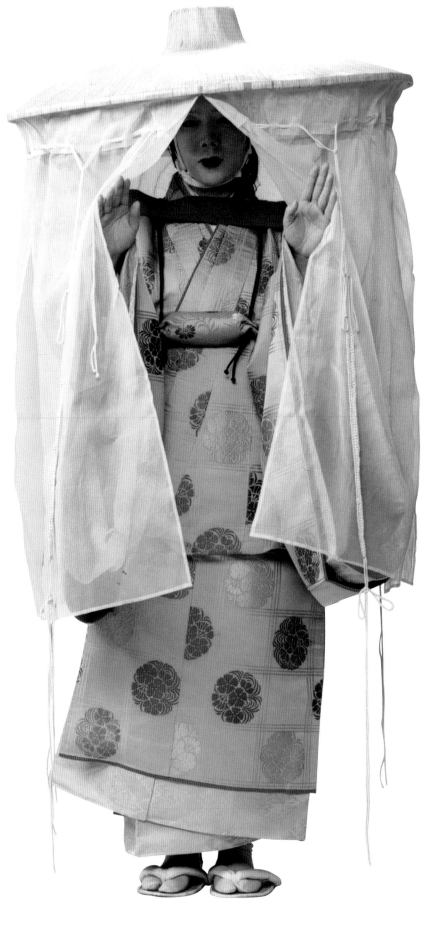

On her way to court, the lady has met with a male acquaintance and so raises her veil to reveal her face in order to exchange a word or two of traditional greeting.

SAMURAI HITATARE
Mid-Kamakura period

By this time, the form of the kikutoji seam reinforcements had changed the shape of the hitatare. Its original "flower shaped" style had become one that required the use of knotted and tied cord. These included those on the sleeves, were the cords were used to shorten and restrict the sleeve when in combat, even though the cord at the lower end of the hakama was retained.

Here, the footwear is rather unusual for a samurai, as he wears tabi socks and *zohri* sandals.

The "three-triangle" motif used to pattern the garment is indicative that the wearer is a member of the Hojo family. In fact, there were two famous Hojo families in Japanese history. One was the Hojo of the Kamakura regency period and the other the Hojo from Odawara in the Sengoku era. The use of somewhat larger triangles in the former's motif assists in identifying both the wearer's family and historical period.

Samurai of this period usually carried a fan, either tucked into the belt or hand-held. It served not only its normal, cooling function but was also used in emergency in deflecting any sudden thrust by an enemy sword. Later, and in the latter context, a general's fan would sometimes have an iron rim when carried in a campaign or at camp.

He is wearing the somewhat straighter tachi sword of the Heian and Kamakura periods.

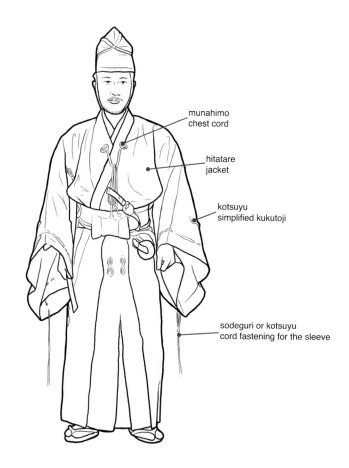

munahimo
chest cord

hitatare
jacket

kotsuyu
simplified kukutoji

sodeguri or kotsuyu
cord fastening for the sleeve

Above and right: *Right and left side views reveal the clear shape of the eboshi cap, adapted so that a rear protrusion can retain the traditional samurai hair knot, the trailing sleeve cords, and zohri sandals.*

Right: *The Hojo family black triangular motif is especially prominent against the hitatre background color in this rear view of the costume. The use of any lower fastening cord of the hakama had been discontinued.*

Below: *With sword just drawn—maybe to protect himself—using just the right hand, but perhaps only for show as the sleeves are not tiled back for immediate action and the tabi socks are without the usual sandals. The fan remains tucked into his obi belt.*

LADY'S WALKING-OUT COSTUME AND FEMALE SERVANT'S DRESS
Kamakura period

Differing in style from the outfit seen earlier (pages 42-45), the *utiki* here is not worn as a coat. Instead, it is used as cape, although its belt remains fastened at the shoulder. However, the lady is still wearing a second utiki in the normal way, under the outer cape utiki, with an amulet hung around her neck.

The utiki cape could be fastened (as right) but also for left open and merely held over the head for brief outings only, as travel from, say Kyoto to Kamakaru, would have

been difficult on horseback. For such walks, she would have worn grass sandals with thick, cloth-covered straps and would have been accompanied by her female servant or maid.

The servant's kosode, or short-sleeve kimono, was the result of underwear that was gradually adopted as home dress and eventually became the usual and common everyday wear.

Her *mo* style skirt has no belt and instead is tied on at the waist on her right side.

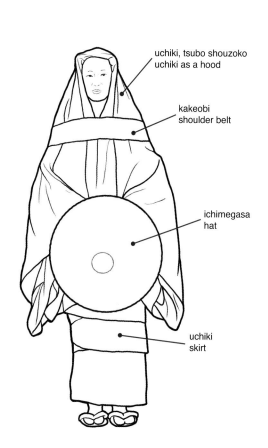

uchiki, tsubo shouzoko
uchiki as a hood

kakeobi
shoulder belt

ichimegasa
hat

uchiki
skirt

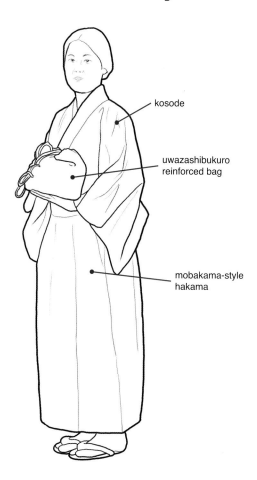

kosode

uwazashibukuro
reinforced bag

mobakama-style
hakama

Left: *A view of the utiki costume form the rear, with the cape drawn over the head.*

Right: *The utiki in cape form, but held open for a short excursion, revealing the lady's amulet suspended around her neck.*

Above: *Whilst out walking with her maid, the lady meets a samurai who engages her in polite and formal conversation.*

Left: *The servant's short-sleeve kimono is worn as a jacket and she carries her mistress's folded and wrapped utiki cape.*

SUIKAN COSTUME
Heian to Muromachi period

Suikan apparel was similar to the aristocrats' kariginu hunting clothes. Around the neck and sleeves, the tunic was unsewn at the front but had a sleeve cord. The main difference between the suikan and kariginu was that the former was shorter in length and could be tucked inside the hakama if required. In reality, the kariginu was regarded as the aristocrat's sporting outfit, while the suikan was usually worn by commoners, juvenile aristocrats and upper-class samurai.

The suikan had a neck cord fastening, although the neck was often folded down for comfort in relaxation and, in which case, the cord was hung over the right shoulder, down to left hip and tied to the chest. Its wrist cord was usually highly decorated.

This youthful samurai is wearing the haramaki armor and tachi sword. His hakama is similar to a hitatare but with the lower part tied.

His use of face make-up might indicate that he has an important social meeting coming up, such as a royal audience or the carrying and delivery of a message from the Emperor himself.

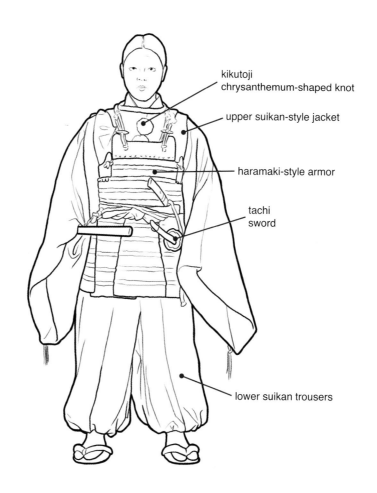

kikutoji
chrysanthemum-shaped knot

upper suikan-style jacket

haramaki-style armor

tachi
sword

lower suikan trousers

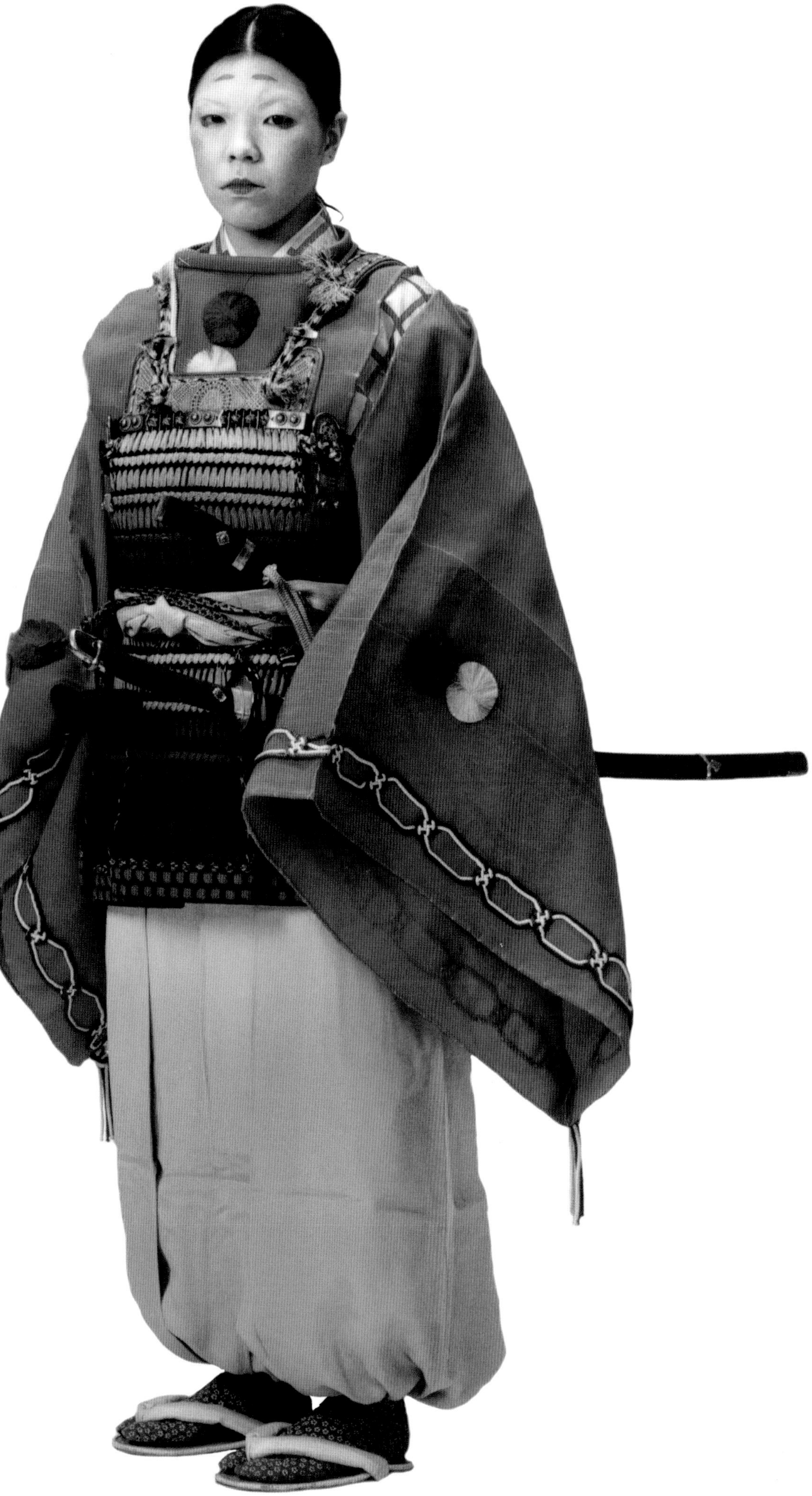

Left and below: *Front and rear views of the young samurai in the haramaki armor and wearing a tachi sword over the suikan costume. His hair is worn long and without the top knot*

A view to show the very full sleeves of the suikan. Also, the neck cord fastening can be seen, although the neck of the garment here, as was often the case, is folded down for comfort and the cord was hung over the right shoulder. Such sleeve decoration was called kikukuri and was made almost exclusively for a male under the age of fifteen and could not fasten.

Below: With the his armor and weapons laid out before him, the young man is wearing the suikan in the tarikubi or neck-drop style with sleeves removed and folded back, although the green cord across his chest, from the left shoulder to the right hip is, alas, not historically accurate.
.

Above: Rear of the armor showing the shoulder fastenings

In these modern photographs of a replica haratare armor, some of the shoulder cords show signs of wear, and tear, looking rather frayed and tassel-like.

Details of the front of the replica armor (right) and a look at the inside when opened up (below).

DAIMON HITATARE
Kamakura to Murohamchi period

The daimon was a variation of the hitatare and nearly always carried a large version of the family crest as an integral part of its design. This daimon is patterned with a crest made up of gentian flowers and a bamboo leaf, which represents the Minamoto family.

The basic construction of the daimon was that of the hitatare, but it became much more an item of rather formal dress and thus was never worn as working dress or beneath armor. As a result, the kikutoji had become a cord and a sleeve strap, hanging as accessory and the lower strap cord was omitted.

Sometimes aristocrats wore both the hitatare and diamon. In which case the hitatare would have a lining; but this samurai has merely the daimon as the upper layer.

Beneath the daimon, the wearer had first to dress in two layers of hitoe style undershirts with the usual open armpit design (see over page).

This daimon is specifically from the Muromachi period, although its description in novels and depiction in movies can often be inaccurate through negligence or genuine ignorance.

daimon-style hatatare with family crest

Above and right: *Rear and side view with a clear view of the sleeves and hanging straps. The fan is held in the right hand as a symbol of office.*

Above and right: *The two layers of hitoe-style under-shirts that were worn beneath the daimon, with the open armpits and upper undershirt without any cord or straps.*

HUNTING OUTFIT
Kamakura to Muromachi period

This upper-class samurai costume includes the suikan as worn for hunting. The round neck is folded down in a style called *tarikubi*.

His hat is made of straw and top protrusion accommodates his tie knot hair. He put on the left arm guard, which is not armored heavily. He only needed to protect his left arm from the bowstring.

The disc hanging from the sword is a spare bowstring holder and a required item for any archer.

The rather fine pair of gloves would usually have been made from leather.

When hunting, arrows were usually carried in a container called an *utsubo*. However, in fast-moving situations or rapid shooting practice, samurai needed to use an ebira quiver or just arrow stuck into the obi belt at the back.

He is wearing a pair of deer-hide chaps-like over-trousers and leather shoes rather than grass sandals.

The top of the straw hat contains his hair knot as well as an eboshi cap.

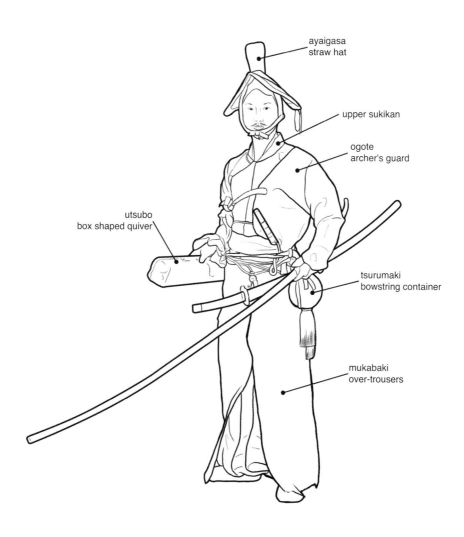

ayaigasa
straw hat

upper sukikan

ogote
archer's guard

utsubo
box shaped quiver

tsurumaki
bowstring container

mukabaki
over-trousers

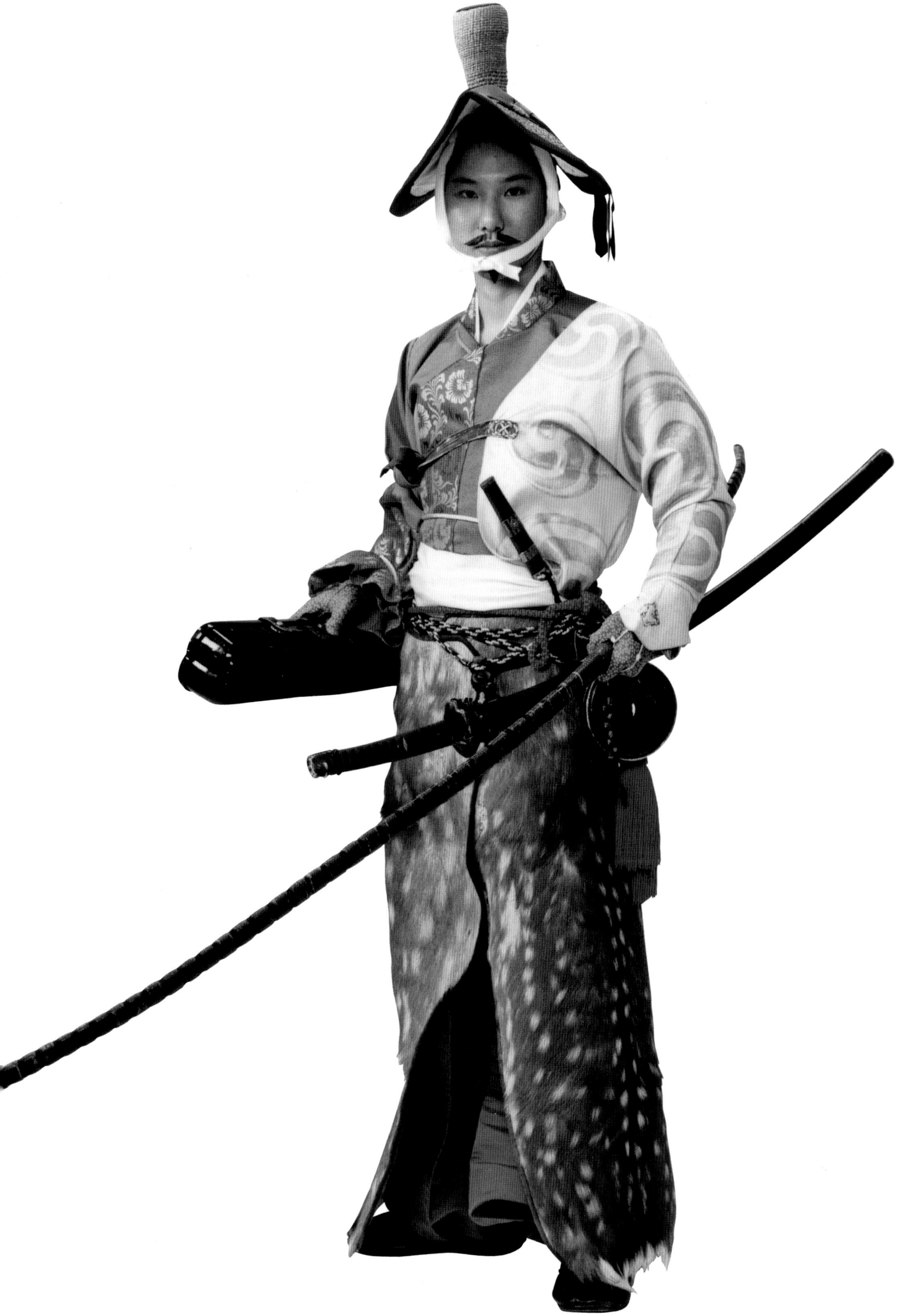

Left: Ready for the hunt, having discarded the awkward utobo and instead having an arrow tucked into the rear of his white obi belt ready for his bow.

Right: A detailed rear view showing the fastening of the deer-hide over-trousers.

Above: The green leather gloves in detail along with the decorated utsobo arrow container.

Right: Now carrying all of his weapons in his left hand, the young hunter has exchanged his straw hat for a soft eboshi cap.

YOUNG FARM GIRL
Kamakura to Edo period

This kosode-style kimono is almost identical to a modern kimono other than in its fabric. She also wears a hemp apron and grass sandals with thick strap.

The costume and incidents depicted here and the following pages are more-or-less based upon how she would have appeared at the time of an old story. It may well have also included a samurai very much like the young man out hunting as in the previous pages.

The tale tells of how the farm girl presented a Japanese globe flower and a short poem to a young samurai when, out hunting, he called at the farmer's house in order to rborrow or hire a *mino* straw raincoat.

She intimated that she was sorry for being so poor that she could not even lend him such a humble item, but presenting the seedless globe flower as a metaphor for the lack of raincoat, as the Japanese for "seedless" is very similar in sound tio that meaning "no rain coat".

However, he failed to grasp its meaning at the time, and when he returned home, one of his retainers had to explain to him what poem meant.

sagegami
hairstyle

katabira
summer hitoe jacket
of silk or linen

kakeyumaki
apron

Below: The young peasant girl presents the youthful samurai hunter with the seedless globe flower as a symbol of both her poverty but willingness to help a traveller in need.

Left: The young samurai, ashamed of his ignorance, began to study diligently the old traditions and their significance. Later, as the story goes, the same young hunter became a very famous samurai and founded the Edojo castle that stands to this day, in the center of Tokyo. Whether a true account from the time or a later fiction, it is as good a legend as any and just as hard to verify!

KOGUSOKU LIGHT ARMOR
Kamakura to Mumomachi period

In camp, a samurai commander is seated, ready for battle and wearing kogusoku light armor. This consisted of a hitatare-based outfit with leg protectors, shoes, a left arm guard, a right side arm and cap. Being no longer an archer, he has no need to remove his left inner sleeve beneath its guard.

His eboshi hat is folded into a form of cap, held in place by a headband, called a *hachimaki*, and tied at the forehead. A neck guard was regarded as being an optional extra of the kogusoku style.

He is armed with a dagger but has no sword and he would have gone into battle bearing a naginata as his weapon.

His bearskin shoes are typical footwear of a leader or mounted samurai of the period.

The ohyoroi was box-shaped in construction and functioned to protect the body, with the flat side-plate flat taking the most of any impact in battle.

His gauntlets consist of just three plates, a rather simple construction compared to those worn in later periods.

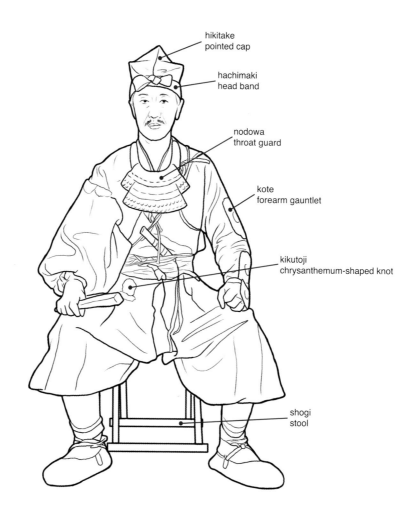

hikitake
pointed cap

hachimaki
head band

nodowa
throat guard

kote
forearm gauntlet

kikutoji
chrysanthemum-shaped knot

shogi
stool

Above: *Carrying the fan in his right hand as a of authority throughout the land, he would not have given battle unarmed, despite the obvious absence of any sword. In fact, his preferred weapon would almost certainly have been the naginata, along with the small dagger or knife tucked into the white obi belt.*

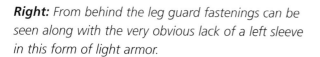

Right: *From behind the leg guard fastenings can be seen along with the very obvious lack of a left sleeve in this form of light armor.*

Left: *When seen from the right-hand side, the box-shaped ohyoroi shows much more clearly how its flat side protected the wearer and took the brunt of any impact taken in battle. The particular folded-back shape of the eboshi is also most obvious in this view.*

Right: *When seated and seen from the left, the three-plate decorated gauntlet is clearly visible on the left forearm. More detail of the bearskin footwear can be made out along with their ties and fastenings.*

LADY'S WALKING-OUT COSTUME
Muromachi to Sengoku period

This elegant lady is wearing a kosode-style kimono, with another kosode worn over her head as form of cape or hood.

This style of katugu was sometimes referred to as *kazuku* and included a narrow form of the traditional obi belt.

By this time, the techniques of fabric printing had developed considerably, enabling cloth to be produced with elaborate decorative patterns, as is evident in this fine outfit.

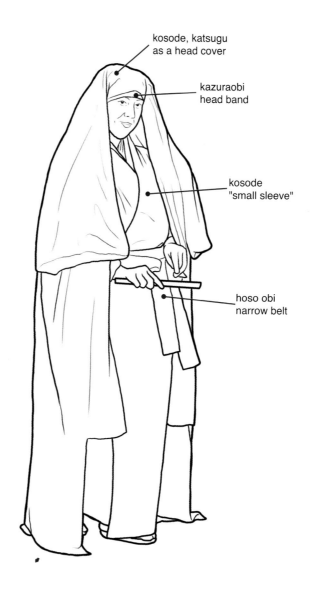

kosode, katsugu
as a head cover

kazuraobi
head band

kosode
"small sleeve"

hoso obi
narrow belt

WARRIOR MONK AND RETAINER
Late Heian to Nanbokucho period

Following the introduction of Buddhism to Japan (by the Chinese teacher Lanqi Daolong in 1246), Buddhist temples acquired their own considerable lands under the protection of Emperor.

By and large, temples sited around the old capitals of Nara and Kyoto behaved as if they were independent colonies. They maintained their strength and power rigorously and did not hesitate to threaten any enemy by force. In effect, the power and rule in Japan was tripartite: the Emperor, the temples and the samurai.

In the manor-style temples, the role and life of a monk began to be integrated with the positions and functions of others, such as those of an artisan, merchant or farmer.

This monk is possibly receiving a report from a retainer, but the characteristic white mask shows that he is an armed monk and wears an haratare armor under his monk's robe or hoi.

In contrast, the poorer retainer is dressed more like a farmer-warrior.

The naginata was undoubtedly the monks' favorite weapon although the mace or staff was also a persuasive addition to his armory. When armed this way, he wears *habaki* leg guards and a typical pair of wooden sandals or *geta*. Normally, geta had

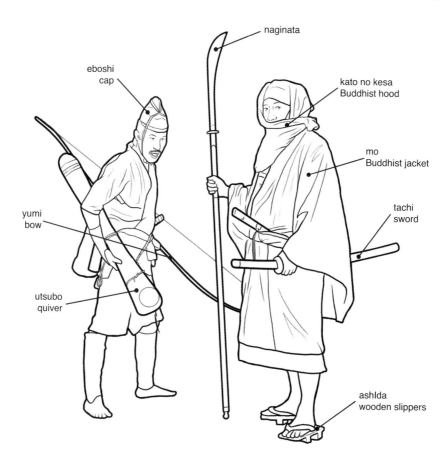

naginata

eboshi
cap

kato no kesa
Buddhist hood

mo
Buddhist jacket

yumi
bow

tachi
sword

utsubo
quiver

ashIda
wooden slippers

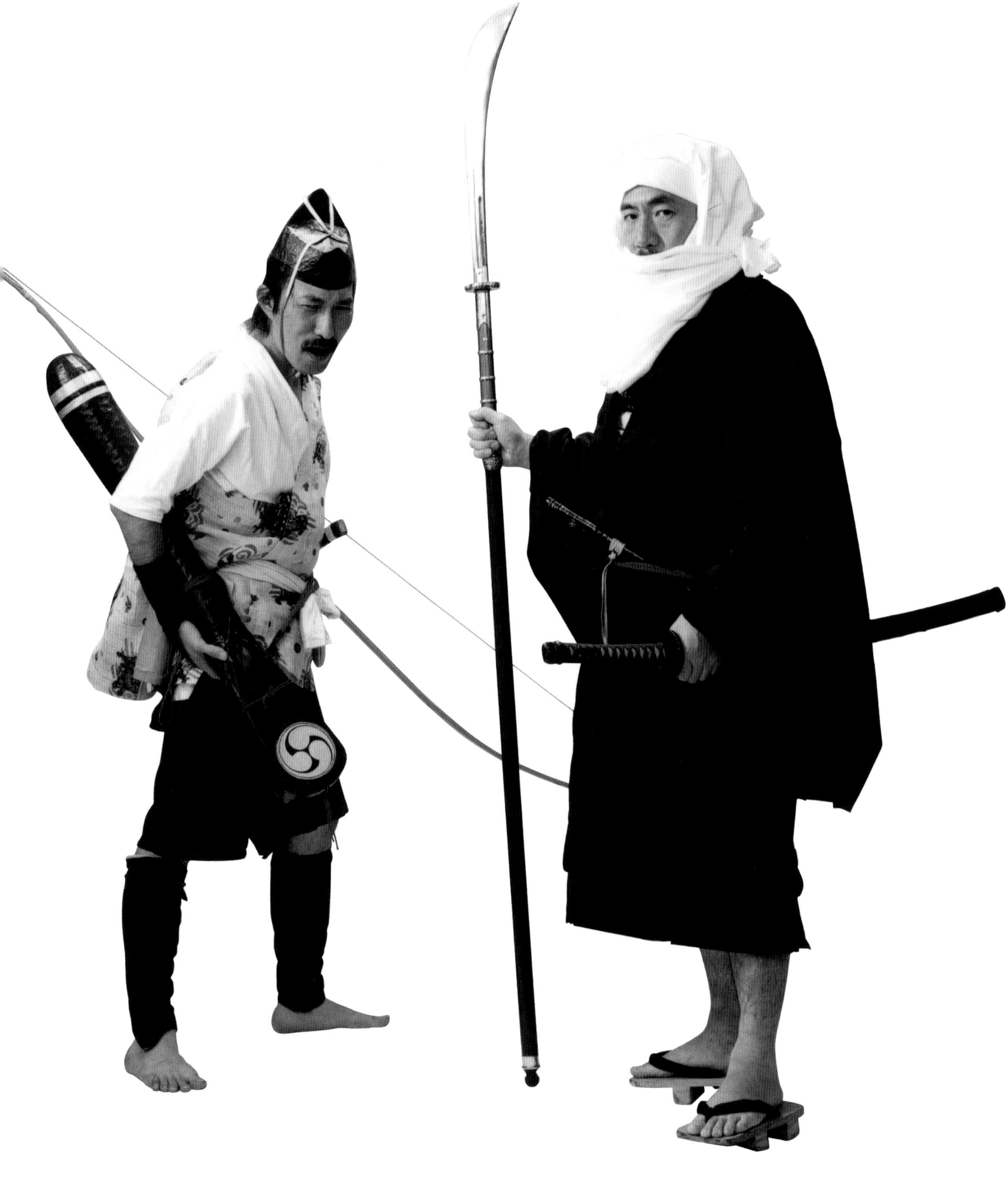

two horizontal bars as grips across the sole, but some monks living in mountainous regions wore multi-gripped versions in such difficult terrain.

The archer (*below*) might be a hunter in the service of the warrior-monk and their association a result of the reduced attention to distinctions of social position that emerged in the Kamakura period and on into the Sengoku era. Some of the reasons for this were of straightforward necessity. Even the samurai needed to engage in agricultural activity when they were poor. So, even if serving as a soldier when required, the warrior had to turn his hand to whatever he could in peacetime in order to make a living.

Samurai were often hired by the lords of the larger manors in order to act as guards. When this role grew to be powerful and actually challenged the samurai government, the individual "renegade" came to be regarded as a bandit or a villain, called an *akuto*.

The warrior monk with his other weapons, in place of the poled naginata. With his staff, he stands defiant (above) and is distinctly threatening when brandishing the mace (left), in both cases wearing habaki leg guards and wooden geta sandals.

ASHIGARU SOLDIER
Muromachi period

The ashigaru, or light foot soldiers, first appeared in the Muromachi period as auxiliary combatants. Most ashigaru came from the ranks of the jobless, but included some struggling, lower-class samurai. In practice, becoming part of the ashigaru was one of the easiest ways to earn some money!

Thus, they were hired as a form of mercenary by samurai leaders and were heavily involved in what was the almost continuous battle of that period. For example, during the Ohnin wars, both sides hired ashigaru extensively and amalgamated them into their standing forces. There were two main factors involved in their emergence on the scene and role in battle.

Firstly, the samurai leaders wanted to limit the action of their principal fighting corps to decisive battles only, Thus, it became essential to keep these crack forces intact.

Secondly, the, continuous battle that raged almost destroyed all of the industry in and around the city of Kyoto. Losing a job as a result of this meant that many men became robbers or beggars and willing to do just about anything to get a job and earn some sort of living. So, there was a ready pool of men for hire, not only by the samurai but also by the powerful manor-owning aristocrats, the temple lords and such like, all of whom needed such manpower to protect their lands.

This is an early-period ashigaru armed with a naginata. He is wearing a soft eboshi cap and a light blue kosode. The face guard, or *hatsupuri* (sometimes called *happuri*), only covered the cheek and forehead. The long lower edge of the kosode was lifted and tucked into the obi for the better

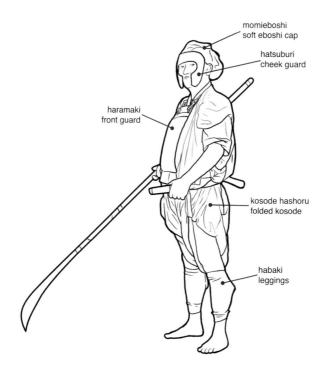

momieboshi
soft eboshi cap

hatsuburi
cheek guard

haramaki
front guard

kosode hashoru
folded kosode

habaki
leggings

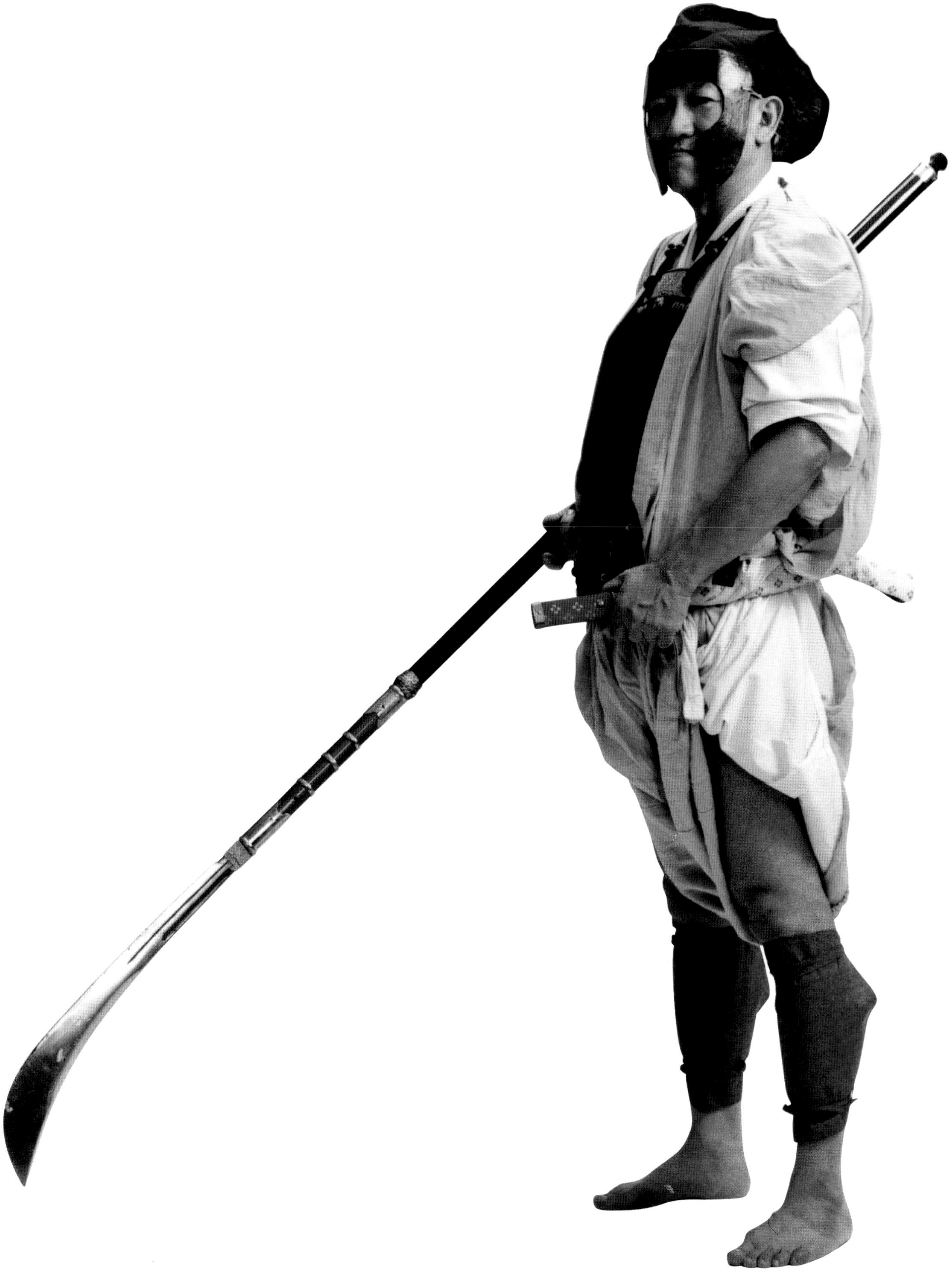

footwork. His armor is of the haraake type and both leg and arm guards were also worn. Carrying a sword was rare for the ashigaru, as swordsmanship was rather a limited skill and tended to be confined only to the samurai. Because of this, a dagger was the only weapon of self-defensive or for the severing of an enemy's head.

Ashigaru were still fighting barefoot as late as the seventeenth century when grass sandals were adopted; but even by then these were very short and covered only the toes on their upper side.

Right: *From the front, showing the leg guards and the folded and tucked style of hakama or kosode adopted in battle.*

Right and below: *Two ways of carrying or holding the naginata and with front haraake and happuri face guards in place and the very obvious a lack of a left sleeve in this form of light armor.*

KAWAZUTUMI YOROI ARMOR
Kamakura to Muromachi period

A lower-class bowman wearing a simple white kosode beneath kawazutumi yoroi leather-covered armor. It is of domaru-style in its origin and incorporates large shoulder guards.

The expanding and extensive need for protection necessitated the recycling of old armor and the sane discarded lamella armor were regarded as being particularly precious by armorers.

Similarly, broken armor was also repaired and covered with leather so as not to show any old indentations and signs of battle.

The warrior also wears the archery characteristic kote on his left, and is carrying sword, its scabbard reinforced with cane. When using his bow, he would have pushed back the sword into a more vertical position for easier firing. The large sode guard is of domaru style and protected any attack by sharp shooters

The rather arbitrary, overall style of his armament and equipment that may suggest he belongs to akuto or bandit groups that appeared in late Kamakura period and wore anything that served for better protection.

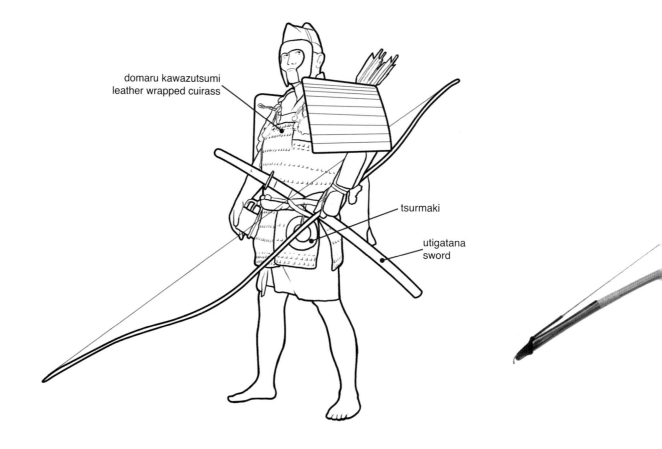

domaru kawazutsumi
leather wrapped cuirass

tsurmaki

utigatana
sword

AKUTO SAMURAI AND RETAINER
Nanbokucho period

Generally, in feudal Japanese society, samurai were in fief and more or less belonged to their master. However, after the thirteenth-century Mongol invasion of Japan, lower class samurai suffered some serious economic problems. Although they had repelled the invasion, many were reduced to depending on loans and lost their lands.

They defied both local administrators as well the samurai government in Kamakura, challenging all forms of existing authority. These were the akuto, the bandit samurai, and very different from the later samurai called ronin. The latter were very much individuals in outlook and activities, whereas the akuto bandit functioned very much as an independent and organized economic group. Their emergence was a sure sign that the centralized authorities in Kyoto and Kamakura were began to crumble.

This akuto is wearing a leader's helmet, obviously plundered from the enemy. Yet, his armor is rather of the somewhat humble haratare, while his retainer wears a kosode with short hakama or yonobakama. Both wear a happuri face guard.

The retainer carries the longer form of sword that appeared in the Nanbokucho period, a brief two-year spell of imperial restoration between the Kamakura and Muromachi periods.

The form of battle in this period had become one of siege warfare and even samurai leaders had to fight on foot. Consequently, such big sword was very convenient with which to halt a mounted

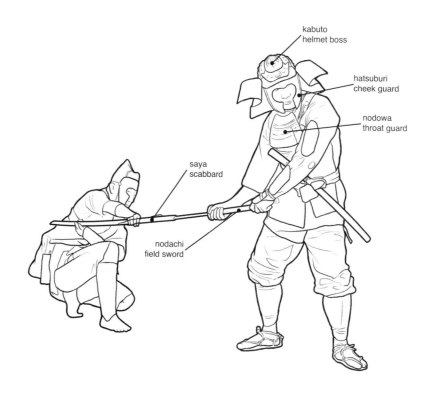

kabuto
helmet boss

hatsuburi
cheek guard

nodowa
throat guard

saya
scabbard

nodachi
field sword

samurai charge by chopping off the legs of the oncoming horses!

Such a warrior master always needed a sword carrier with him (*right*).

After the conflict, the scabbard was often disposed of. It usually became very battle worn and warped to the degree that the sword could never be returned to be housed in it.

On his back, the barefoot retainer carries a bamboo canteen on his back (visible to the rear of his hip) for his master's refreshment on the battleground.

The akuto retainer in his kosode, yonobakama and hap-puri face guard. He holds his master's long nanbokucho sword with pride.

SUOH HITATARE
Muromachi to Sengoku period

There are always two concurrent strands in the evolution of costume. One is the tendency to adopt the costume easiest to wear for working. The other is to adapt lower-class costume and then adopt it as formal dress.

These were developments clearly evident in the history of Japanese costume in both aristocratic society and among the samurai class

Initially, the hitatare was solely the wear of a commoner. However, it was a garment that proved to be convenient as everyday working dress for the samurai and was then adopted as formal dress.

In essence, the suoh is a simplified variation of hitatare in which the kikutoji, or seam reinforcement, became a form of leather strap necktie and sleeves became completely unrestricted

This samurai's leather strap falls all the way down his front and apart from the samurai knot, the top of his head was shaved in the popular style of this period.

The sides of the suoh and upper part of the hakama were unsewn and the hitatare was usually made from hemp fiber. However, the wonderfully striped example in these photographs was made of silk, in an attempt to depict a very high-class warlord, possibly Takeda Shingen.

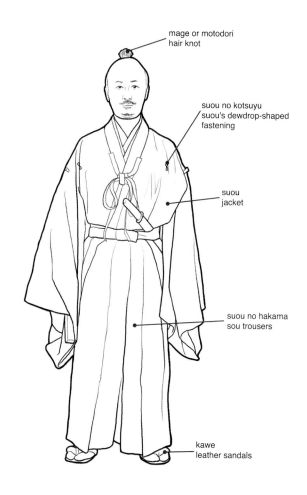

mage or motodori
hair knot

suou no kotsuyu
suou's dewdrop-shaped
fastening

suou
jacket

suou no hakama
sou trousers

kawe
leather sandals

This view from the rear clearly shows the wide, unrestricted sleeves that had become part of the costume by this time.

Below: The warlord carries the symbolic fan in his right hand and his sword is ticked into the obi belt on his left.

Above: Photographic depiction of the sixteenth-century warlord Takeda Shingen of Kai (Yamanshi), the great rival of Uesugi Kenshin of Echigo (Niigata). Only fine silk rather than the more common hemp was appropriate material for such an important and powerful warrior.

LOWER-CLASS KAWAZUTSUMI ARMOR

Muromachi to Sengoku period

This archer holds an arrow with the *kaburaya*, or turnip-shaped, arrowhead, a form with considerable destructive power when striking the enemy. A further enhancement was to hollow out the round arrowhead in order for it to produce a distinct and disturbing, whistling sound when in flight. The container-style quiver was able to contain 12-30 arrows, rather fewer than the alternative ebira type.

His kawazutsumi armor is almost certainly recycled from older armor. It includes a thigh protector and a flexible form of arm guard reinforced with chain mail. The helmet is of the bolted type and attached to the ohyoroi armor, the shikoro side guard having been replaced by a leather one hung with metal lamellae.

The "at alert" stance as adopted by the archer was usual when avoiding an ambush or when he needed to advance on the street or battlefield. It is a stance and form of movement that is very evident in drawn and painted depictions of archers on antique scrolls. However, in this activity it is more likely that the arrows would have just the normal arrowhead. As further armament, he also wears a short sword.

Haramaki armor differed from the domaru type in having its fastenings at the rear (while the former's was always on the right side). This tended to make the

gesanjikoro
plated neck guard

fusubegawazutsumi haratare
smoked leather front guard

haidate
thigh guard

kaburaya
turnip-shaped arrowhead

warrior's back rather vulnerable, so that an oblong plate was added later on in order to cover and protect the gap. Nevertheless, it soon earned itself the disparaging names of "the coward's board."

When not an archer, the samurai would carry both naginata and sword. However, the latter would have been a type called an *uchigatana* and was worn rather differently from previous styles, having been pushed directly into the obi with its blade reversed to that in which a tachi was worn. The sword was housed in a leather scabbard that was lacquered for further protection.

In having to draw a sword quickly and cause immediate damage to an adversary, the samurai began to prefer using the uchigatana rather than the older tachi. In fact, by the Sengoku period, wearing two swords, one long and one short became very popular and hand become standard samurai practice by the Edo period. By that time, only the very high-class samurai and *teppo* (arquebus gunner) hung their swords in the old style.

Right: *Licking the right index finger made for a better grip when ready for action and holding the arrow in the bow.*

Right and below: *A change of role: from archer to barefoot soldier and now armed with both sword and uchigatana-style naginata. Note how the scabbard of this uchigatana-style sword has been pushed directly into the obi belt with its blade reversed against that of the tachi sword. The scabbards were prone to breakage in battle and so were often protectively bound in cane or leather before the lacquer was applied.*

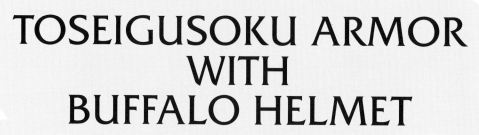

TOSEIGUSOKU ARMOR WITH BUFFALO HELMET
Sengoku period

The old lamella style armor was replaced by plate armor called *toseigusoku*. The *kabuto* itself consisted of six iron plates and was covered by bearskin, as was the cuirass, in order to protect from rain and sunlight.

(Modern re-enactments involving this plate armor, and worn in full summer sunshine, have shown all too clearly that the armor became hot enough to burn the skin.

So, in summer combats of the past, as the samurai or ashigaru often wore the plate armor on the naked body, it is highly likely that they too would have suffered skin burns without any undershirts.)

The helmet's impressive decoration was based on the horns of the water buffalo. They were made of paper and hardened with lacquer, so that while not being quite as heavy as one might imagine, they must have been quite obstructive and their

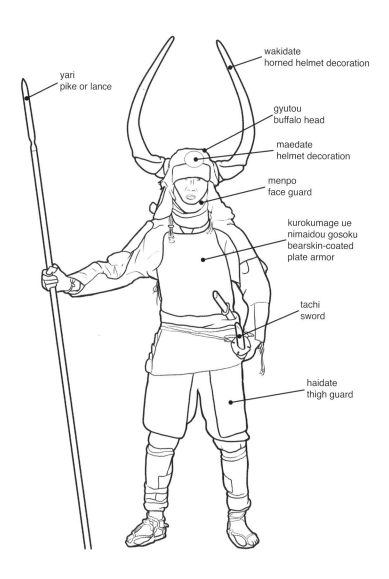

yari
pike or lance

wakidate
horned helmet decoration

gyutou
buffalo head

maedate
helmet decoration

menpo
face guard

kurokumage ue
nimaidou gosoku
bearskin-coated
plate armor

tachi
sword

haidate
thigh guard

paper-based construction meant that breakage in battle was not unusual. However, this not seen to bring about any dishonor to the wearer, but rather added to his prowess.

Carrying, or actually wearing, a flag as part of the armor also appeared in the Muromachi period. It served the double purpose of being a recognition sign in battle and a rather boastful item of self-proclamation.

Although this warrior is wearing a sword and in the tachi manner, use of the pike as a preferred weapon emerged in the Nanbokucho era and it became a common weapon of the samurai in the Muromachi period. Early versions carried a rather short spearhead and were effectively nothing much more than a knife attached to the end of a long pole, and therefore had only a one-side blade. However, by the Muromachi period, the pike became more sophisticated and its spearhead had a triple-edged blade

The ashigaru also later adopted the long pike, but employed it somewhat differently from the samurai, preferring to use it to batter the enemy rather than to poke at them.

Right: *The samurai style of fighting with the pike was very different from its use in western battle practice. Held by the shaft horizontally in the left and right hands (rather as if using a billiards or pool cue) the pike was thrust forward in attack.*

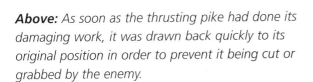

Above: As soon as the thrusting pike had done its damaging work, it was drawn back quickly to its original position in order to prevent it being cut or grabbed by the enemy.

Right: Ready for battle, pike in hand and sword hilt gripped steady, the samurai carries the family or fighting unit recognition flag device fastened at the rear of his armor.

TOSEIGUSOKU ARMOR WITH DEER HELMET
Sengoku period

Another style of horned helmet was based upon deer antlers and was also made of paper with a lacquer coating. It also carried a striking gremlin-like decoration at its front.

At the time, it was quite usual to wear this type of helmet with a face guard. However, this is often omitted in Japanese film and TV dramas in order to show the actor's faces. Nevertheless, the face guard also functioned as fixing for the chinstrap and a throat guard, once worn as a separate item became an integral part and was attached to the bottom of the face guard.

The portable stool is typical of the type used in a samurai war camp.

The golden decoration is, in fact, an imitation of a Buddhist's praying beads. The inherent irony here is that no true Buddhist would not even kill an animal, let alone a fellow human. So for whom might he be praying? For the man he has just killed or just for himself in the hope that he would not go to Hell.

The large shinogate shoulder guards required a folding mechanism similar to that of ohyoroi armor, holding them in place when bending over. However, overall, the

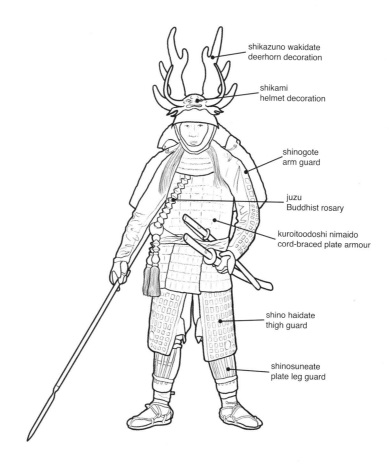

shikazuno wakidate
deerhorn decoration

shikami
helmet decoration

shinogote
arm guard

juzu
Buddhist rosary

kuroitoodoshi nimaido
cord-braced plate armour

shino haidate
thigh guard

shinosuneate
plate leg guard

SAMURAI | ARMS • ARMOR • COSTUME

armor is of the domaru style known as *kon-ito-sugakeodoshi-nimaido*, meaning "braided by blue thread with a simply-sewn, two-part cuirass".

Unusually, the hair-knot of his otherwise shaven head is untied and he is wearing a hachimaki headband tied on the forehead (although it was sometimes tied at the rear).

In the famous illustrated scroll of that chronicles the Mongol War of the thirteenth century, only few warriors are depicted with their hair knot untied.

As the scroll has long been regarded as a very accurate record of that War, it seems likely that until the time of the Mongol invasion, the samurai's practice of wearing the hair knot free and untied beneath a helmet had been somewhat uncommon.

Then, in the mid-to-late Kamakura period, samurai began to untie their hair-knot as common practice before donning a helmet. Nevertheless, other than the hair-knot itself, the rest of the crown was nearly always shaved.

Left and right: *In this outfit, the model is depicting Honda Heihachiro Takakatsu, a famous Tokugawa retainer. Honda Heihachiro made his battlefield debut aged just 13-years-old and went on to fight in battle fifty-seven times without injury.*

Left: *A rear view showing the cord fastenings for the shoulder guards.*

Right: *Without his dear horn helmet but still wearing the protective head band, it can be seen that the top of his head is completely shaved and the rest of his hair hangs loose, rather than tied up in a hair-knot.*

OKEGAWA-DO ARMOR
Sengoku period

The helmet of the okegawa-do armor worn by this samurai is made up of thirty-six, narrow, triangular iron strips and is of a style that first appeared in the Muromachi period, replacing the older type of bolted helmet. The character on the helmet represents "blockade" and is inscribed in gold upon a black background. However, the main feature of the okegawa-do armor is the cuirass with its bolted plate.

Here, the entire outfit, including the very distinctive helmet, is made up of genuine and well-preserved antique armor. In its close-up photographs, the braiding cord has probably been replaced and the armor consists of five plates. It is obvious that only a relatively small man could have worn it, which is very much the case as the average height of Japanese men in the Segoku period was around 5 ft (1.5 m).

The changed, sloping form of the cuirass was influenced by European styles of armor after the introduction of firearms into Japanese combat.

The highly-individual helmet design was a means of identification when its wearer's head was severed as a trophy in battle.

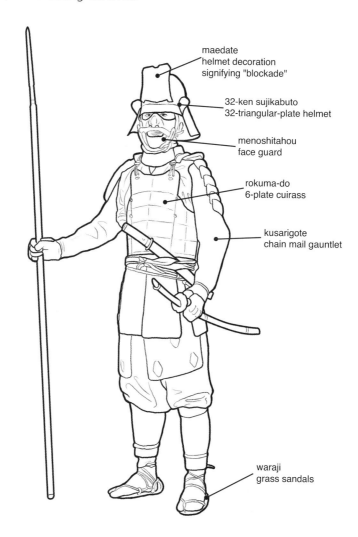

maedate
helmet decoration
signifying "blockade"

32-ken sujikabuto
32-triangular-plate helmet

menoshitahou
face guard

rokuma-do
6-plate cuirass

kusarigote
chain mail gauntlet

waraji
grass sandals

Right: When wearing a jinbaori surcoat, no shoulder guard was worn. But, whatever else, the pike was a "must" for any samurai engaged in battle at this time.

Left: When not in combat, the face guard could be partially unfastened and left over the throat guard.

Left: The rear of the cuirass, showing the affixed gattari rear flagpole holder; however this replica example is missing the socket for the flagpole.

Left: *The full armor, showing the gold-painted character on the bolted helmet, full face guard and its fastening cords, impressive jinbaori surcoat, and leather-gloved hands holding his lowered pike and sword hilt. When a head was severed by an enemy in battle, it would have been covered in blood and dust, so a distinctive helmet such as this could identify its wearer and be presented by the victor to his leader as a trophy.*

Below: *Fully regaled, kneeling in a pledge of honor and duty before battle.*

KATAGINU JACKET
Azuchi-momoyama to Edo period

In effect, the kataginu jacket was the suoh without sleeves. According to the theory of the progressive simplification of costume, the suoh sleeves were shortened for convenience. In practical terms, they were removed from the seam at shoulder, .

Following the pattern of this theory, the Again kataginu had first been worn as daily costume but was later adopted as formal wear.

The kataginu jacket is being worn here over a red and white kosode. The hakama is short with two transverse stripes. In fact, a design featuring two stripes was very popular amongst samurai of this period, and often also featured on the kataginu.

The-called *go-san-no-kiri*, or "five-three" flower markings, feature on his upper shoulder, on the back of obi, on the chest and on each side. The specific crest here is one associated with the famous sixteenth-century warlord Oda Nobunaga.

The replica costume was made according to an old painting created in remembrance of him after his unfortunate death at Honnoji temple at the hands of Akechi Mitsuhide in 1582.

futatsuori no mage
tied and folded hair knot

kataginu
jacket

kosode
under-shirt

hakama
trousers

SAMURAI | ARMS • ARMOR • COSTUME

Above and right: Left and right views reveal the side slits of Oda Nobumaga's hakama.

Left and above: With symbolic fan in the right hand and showing both the twin-white-striped design of the hakama and the family flower markings on the rear of both the kataginu jacket and obi belt.

Below: A seated pose in the replica costume of Oda Nobunaga. The top-knot, moustache, and beard are also based upon a painting of the famous warlord.

CHRISTIAN SAMURAI
Azuchi to Momoyama period

In the mid-1500s, Spanish missionaries brought Christianity to Japan. It was established first in Kyushu, but quickly spread elsewhere. The most influential of the warlords, Oda Nobunaga (see also page 112), adopted and protected the new religion, which was also taken up by many samurai, This was out of choice and not simplyadopted as a fashion in order to imitate and find favor with their leader.

Parallel to the new open attitude towards the spiritual side of western culture, the samurai and merchants were enthusiastic in their welcome of new trade products such as guns, tobacco, clothes, armor, etc.

Consequently, in the Azuchi-Momoyama period, following the years of military conflict and activity, Toyotomi Hideyoshi pacified the warlords and established hegemony over all of Japan.

Thus, even though the contemporary society was not completely peaceful, people began to enjoy life much more fully and in an atmosphere where Japanese costume became very decorative.

This Christian samurai wears a kosode and hakama. The upper jacket, or jimbaori, is sleeveless. It was a development of the samurai battle *dopuku,* or doubuku, that was often showy but also served at one time to protect the body in cold weather, but which later became purely decorative, since the improved modern armor covered more of the upper body and eliminated any need for such under-armor clothes to have any visual appeal.

The neck ruff is of obvious Portuguese influence. The sword is tucked into the obi

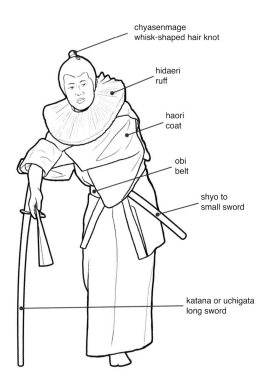

chyasenmage
whisk-shaped hair knot

hidaeri
ruff

haori
coat

obi
belt

shyo to
small sword

katana or uchigata
long sword

rather nonchalantly. Previously, swords had been worn in a more horizontal position, but this made it rather inconvenient to walk in what had by then become the crowded streets of Kyoto or Osaka.

The Momoyama period playboy has adopted a definite attempt to look what was regarded as being "cool" at the time and that was also intended to impress any young females of his acquaintance. The rear of his kosode carries a variation of a popular deign that featured two white bars, here with narrow lines.

In this period, those favoring showy costumes or fond of strange forms of dress, particularly the young people, were called *kabukimono* or "oddballs". The term *kabuki*, as in the unique Japanese art form called kabuki theater, is derived from same word, which simply meant "unusual".

Right: *He may not have been all that good a Christian, but he was crazy about new fashion!*

Left and above: *Front and rear views of the kosode and hakama costume, with the sleeveless upper jimbaori jacket, neck ruff and sword tucked into the obi belt. Deliberately adopting the kabuki-mono "oddball look", his head is unshaven in a style called* chasen-mage, *unlike the samurai style of the period*

LADY'S DAILY COSTUME
Late Sengoku to Azuchi-momoyama period

The continuing simplification of costume applied to women as well as to men and is evident here in a truly gorgeous costume, one of the best amongst all of those kindly supplied from its collection by the Izutus Costume Museum in Kyoto.

The lady wears a green, red and white striped undershirt called an aigi beneath a white kosode that is fastened by a narrow obi, and her uchikake topcoat is untied.

Her hairstyle is typical of the Sengoku to Azuchi-momoyama period and her eyebrows would have been painted in this way. Her long hair is placed under the coat here, but could also be laid outside.

Here, one can see details of the magnificent embroidery, which was often applied to cloth or fabric imported from China and called *karaorimono*. The silk embroidery itself was called *ukiorimono*.

Since importing karaorimono material was quite expensive, the Japanese soon imitated its manufacturing method and their product rapidly became of equivalent or even superior quality to that of the Chinese original.

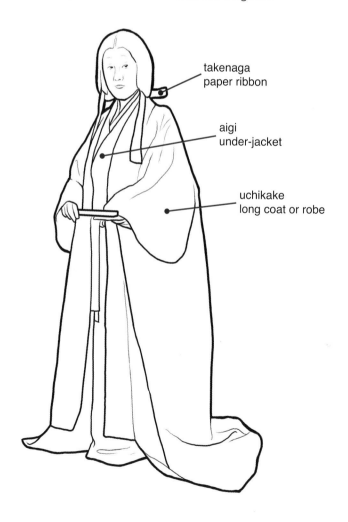

takenaga
paper ribbon

aigi
under-jacket

uchikake
long coat or robe

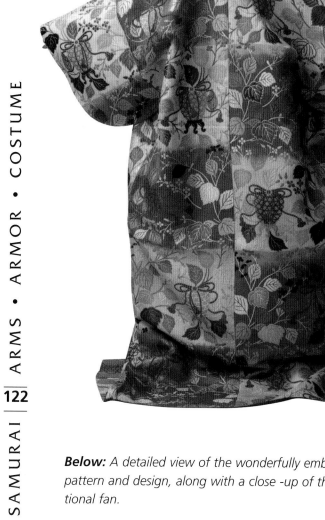

Left and below: *Rear and left side views of the uchicake, with fan in hand and hair worn outside of the coat only at the front.*

Below: *A detailed view of the wonderfully embroidered pattern and design, along with a close -up of the traditional fan.*

Left: *Seen from the rear, the elaborately embroidered costume made of Chinese karaorimono material is seen in all its beauty. The lady's braided hair has two tresses at the front and hangs long down her back.*

Right: *The lady seated, with her right knee folded beneath her, in a style reminiscent of an older Korean posture for women sitting on the floor. Her uchikake here has short sleeves and her hair is worn both over and under the coat.*

LADY'S SUMMER COSTUME
Uchikake-koshimaki style

In summer, a samurai lady removed the upper part of her uchikake and folded it away inside her obi in a style referred to as koshimaki.

It was a style regarded as being formal and became the required costume for the religious dance called *noh*, and which developed into the traditional Japanese drama form that is still performed today.

The costume is also intended to depict Oichi, sister of the warlord Oda Nobunga (see pages 112 and 116).

Her hairstyle, face make-up and painted eyebrows are typical of a high-class lady of this period. However, such women were in a subjugated state. despite their finery. They were regarded by their lords and families almost as strategic weapons, whereby political and military alliances were forged by marriage. If the alliance then broke apart, the woman given in marriage, to what had thus become a rival clan, was virtually doomed for life in all but exceptional cases.

tsukuirmayu
fake eyebrow

suihatsu
drooping hairstyle

aigi
under-jacket

uchikake
robe or coat

hoso obi
narrow belt

Left and below: *The costume as worn in the early noh dance form, with symbolic use of the fan.*

Left: *A model, dressed as Oichi, sister of Oda Nobunga, and seated in the style more usual for males of the time. Her hairstyle and painted eyebrows are typical of this period.*

Below: *A detailed view of the uchiki and uchikake, with its special style fastening of the obi.*

ABARA-DO CUIRASS
Sengoku to early Edo period

These days, it is almost impossible to obtain a complete set of antique samurai armor. Often, even when offered for sale, the helmet and armor come from different sources and antique shop combines them look like a single, original set. However, with some knowledge and a pair of keen eyes, the discrepancy is apparent. Yet, even in museums, some very famous sets of armor attributed to a specific warlord are often, in reality, combinations of different parts from several sources.

More recently, auctions over the Internet have entailed the sale of separate parts of a set of armor, collectors having become more specialized and concentrating only upon certain armor parts, such as helmets, face guards, arm guards, etc. Even in the museum, some very famous sets of armor attributed to a particular warlord is often a mixture of different armor parts.

The model here was photographed in a set of well-preserved domaru armor, the helmet being in the form of a creature called a *shikami* and it has the kind of long horns seen before and worn in a way to protect the forehead.

The flesh-colored, molded face guard has detachable nosepiece guard and a throat guard is hanging from the bottom of the face guard.

The rear part of the helmet was covered

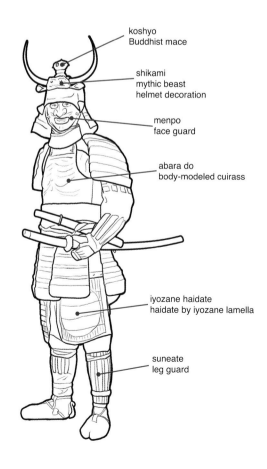

koshyo
Buddhist mace

shikami
mythic beast
helmet decoration

menpo
face guard

abara do
body-modeled cuirass

iyozane haidate
haidate by iyozane lamella

suneate
leg guard

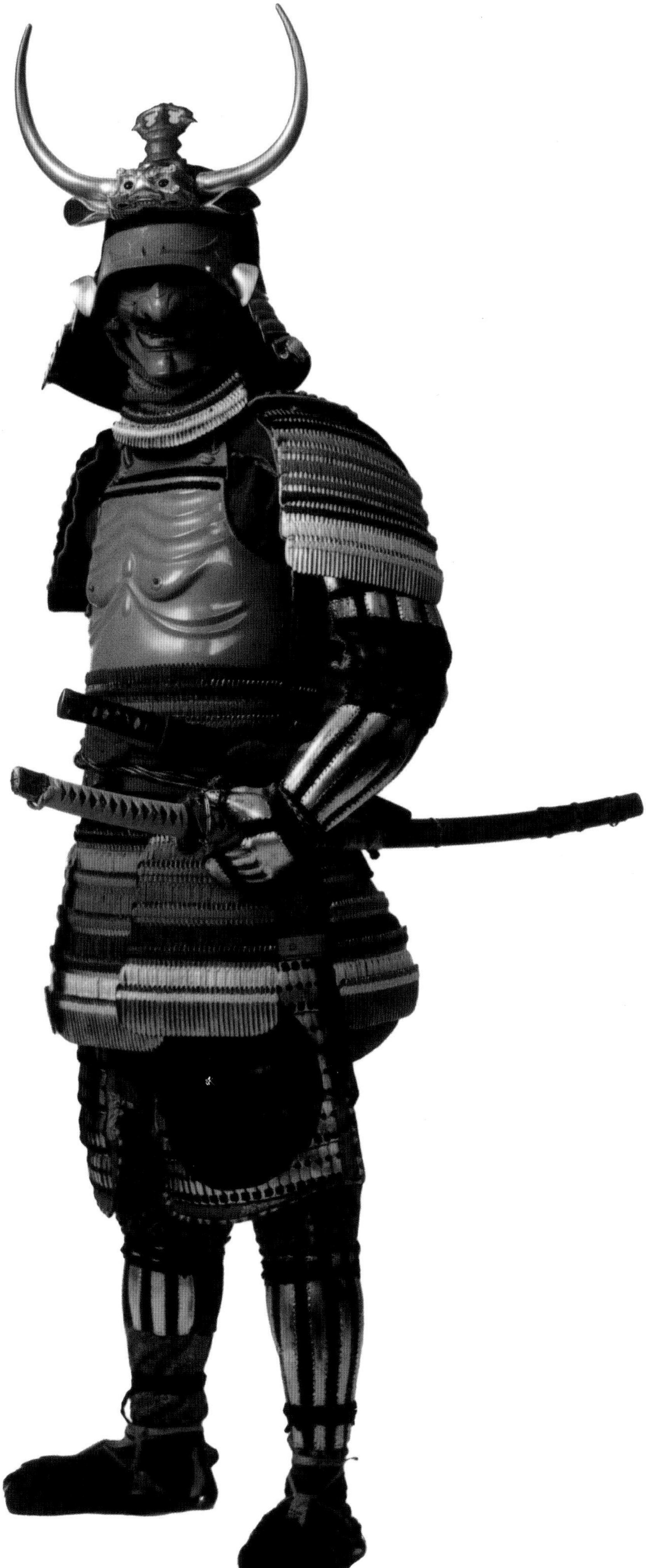

with bearskin to protect the cowl from the direct sunlight or rain; and the sikoro neck guard is made up of a series of small lamellae, each row braided with differently colored cords.

The kusazuri is also made of gold-colored lamella, as is the thigh guard but decorated with a large, dark blue roundel painted over it. The sword is hung in tachi style.

The flesh-colored cuirass was embossed in order to resemble the samurai's muscular chest. This is a style that was also used my the Roman armies, but the samurai form of it showed more prominence to the ribs than to muscle, rather imitating the shape of an older old man's chest.

The warrior's kusazuri hanging thigh guard is constructed similarly to his shikoro and shoulder guard.

Below: Detailed side view of the helmet showing the protective bearskin and neck guard at the rear.

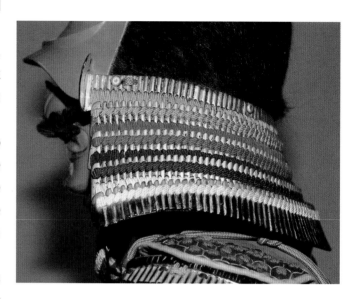

Above: A close-up of the gold-painted arm guard showing how the usual strap for the middle finger has been split open as being no longer in use.

Left: Detail of the kusazuri hanging thigh and front guard.

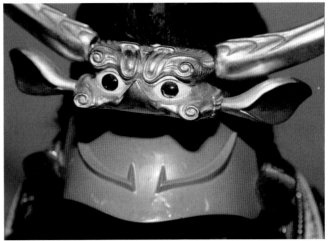

Above: Detail of the helmet showing the decoration in the form of the mythical creature called a shikami.

Left and below left: Seated rather unusually but giving a clear view of his flesh-colored cuirass intended to resemble the bare human chest.

Below: Also flesh-colored and molded, the face guard had a detachable nosepiece guard and a throat guard is hanging from the bottom of the face guard.

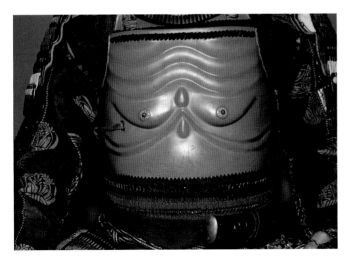

SAMURAI PLUNDERER
Sengoku to Azuchi-momoyama period

In medieval Japan, most villages and communities maintained their own defenses, with the samurai government sanctioning their right to do so. In time of war, many villagers, including samurai, were often drafted or actually volunteered for military service. After the battles were over, they returned home only to find that they then had to defend their village from plundering raids by other samurai and ashigaru who had become deserters.

Furthermore, the journeys on their way to enlist or in returning home from battle, vanquished or otherwise, often proved to be just as dangerous as their subsequent defensive roles. They had to pass through what was effectively "no man's land" and were often attacked and ambushed by bounty hunters. This was so common that it even took place within their home territories too.

Often though, the villagers regarded the retreating samurai bandits as nothing more than a nuisance. Sadly, although a classic movie, Akira Kurosawa's famous depiction of such a situation in the hiring of a defensive gang in "The Seven Samurai" would have been a somewhat rare occurrence. (However, the story line proved so strong, however that it was transferred to the American West and became even better known as "The Magnificent Seven".)

The fact of the matter is that in the Sengoku period, a farmer was not only the

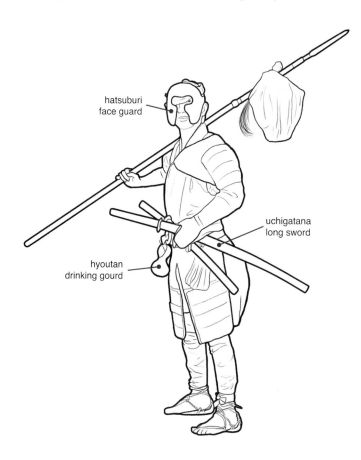

hatsuburi
face guard

uchigatana
long sword

hyoutan
drinking gourd

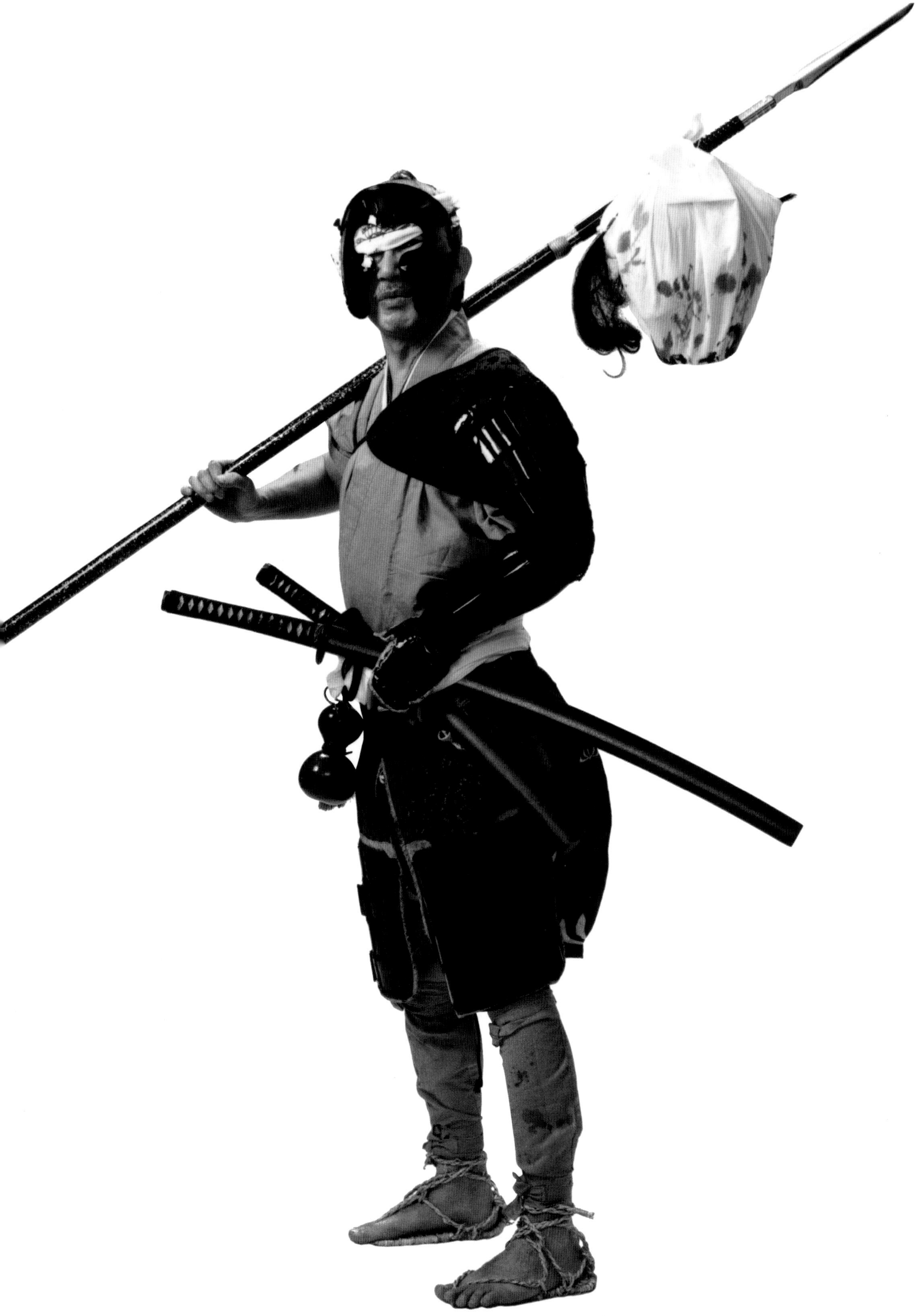

person who worked the land and tended the animals of his village, he was also often a warrior or and ashigaru. Self-defense really was the watchword and principle of a Sogoku-era village.

Whatever else, it was very much a time of raiding, plundering, ambush and theft on the battlefield.

Below: With his happuri face guard, this seated warrior might well be a battlefield robber and have taken the gourd after battle. When fighting, the gourd would have been used as canteen, a favorite type of water bottle that appeared in the Muromachi period.

Above: The lightly armed samurai is carrying his loot after ambushing a retreating samurai. He is clad in a kosode and short hakama (or yonobakama), wearing his sword the uchigatana way. His only real protective clothing consists of just a gauntlet and haidate thigh guard.

Left: *Taking some refreshment, but what is the likelihood that the stolen gourd now contains not water, but sake?*

Right: *A more detailed view of the short, patterned haidate.*

HARAMAKI ARMOR
Sengoku period

A daimyo, or samurai warlord, wearing a suit of haramaki armor and caries the traditional staff fan of office. His white hood (see over page) indicates that he is also a Buddhist monk.

Although lacking any neck guard, he wears a *nodowa* throat protector and, lower down, the domaru has a seven-row kusazuri thigh protector.

The haramaki rear is reinforced centrally by an *okubyo-ita* or "coward's board" and the sode shoulder guard is not as large as the ohsode, being slightly curved in order to fit the upper arm, although it still has the mizunomi-no-o device as the ohyoroi.

Sitting on the stool, he depicts the warlord Uesugi Kenshin of Exchigo (or Niigata) province and great rival of Takeda Shingen (see also pages 92-95). He is attended by a sword bearer/helmet bearer and so is not wearing his tachi sword.

When wearing the hood without helmet, the helmet is attached with parasol-like shikoro. The rear board and sode of the haramaki armor had a fixing device of three, colored cords that were used to braid the lamellae.

The watagami shoulder straps were often of white leather and decorated with small designs. Two cords, with buttons on each watagami, served as straps for attaching it to the sode.

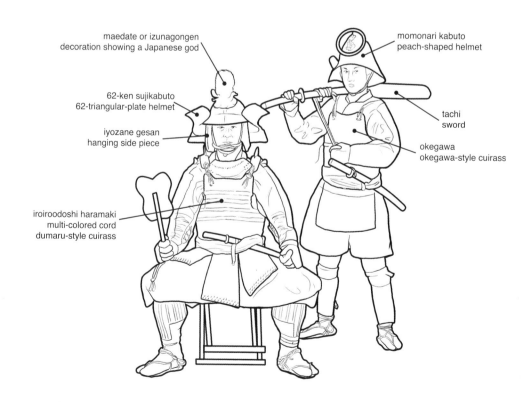

maedate or izunagongen
decoration showing a Japanese god

momonari kabuto
peach-shaped helmet

62-ken sujikabuto
62-triangular-plate helmet

tachi
sword

iyozane gesan
hanging side piece

okegawa
okegawa-style cuirass

iroiroodoshi haramaki
multi-colored cord
dumaru-style cuirass

Below: Uesugi Kenshin's boy attendant in the role of helmet bearer of the un-lacquered helmet, with its prominent gold-colored depiction of a Japanese god and two-layered neck guard.

Right: *Wearing a helmet under the white Buddhist hood, with standard raised and fan of office at the ready, Uesugi Kenshin is ready for one of his five famous battles with Takeda Shingen. The most famous, their fourth, near Kawanakjima was recorded by the Edo-period Kyogunkan chronicler, a scholar of the Takeda military school. Modern historians regard his account of the thousands of deaths as being somewhat exaggerated and biased.*

Left: *Detailed view of the rear protection, the so-called "coward's board" and red sode cords with the fixing loop and decorated white leather shoulder straps.*

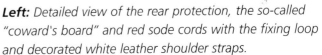

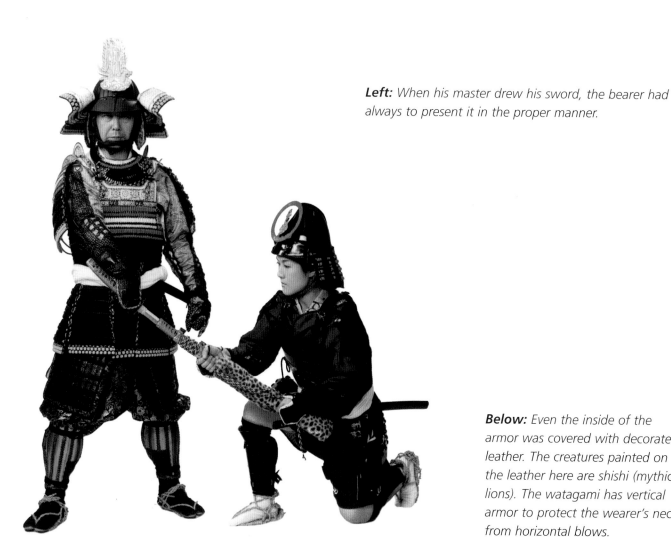

Left: When his master drew his sword, the bearer had always to present it in the proper manner.

Below: Even the inside of the armor was covered with decorated leather. The creatures painted on the leather here are shishi (mythical lions). The watagami has vertical armor to protect the wearer's neck from horizontal blows.

Right: *The helmet view seen from the rear and above. It was made up of thirty-six thin, metal triangles and its rear tying cord matches the color of those at the back of the cuirass.*

Below: *After his master had used the sword the attendant bearer had to wipe away any blood with a piece of paper.*

II FAMILY AKAZONAE RED ARMOR
Early to late Edo period

Afurther example of antique armor , and this time associated with the Ii family, who were retainers to the Tokugwa and who had merged with the Itagaki family (in turn, retainers of the Takeda). The Ii family thus adopted the Itagaki red armor and helmet as their own and became famous for their courage and fighting abilities.

At the famous Battle of Sekigahara in 1600, Ii Naomasa pursued a Shimazu force that was attempting to disengage from the battle and flee the field. In so doing, he killed Shimazu Toyohisa but, in turn, was shot by a retreating Shimazu gunner.

Naomas's outfit was always red in color and the red flag his banner. In its center there was often painted the character that represented the Ii name (and which resembled the modern symbol of #).

At the rear is the gattari flag pole container, but also shows signs that while the red under shirt and hakama are a little too large for the re-enactor, the armor itself is probably somewhat too small for him.

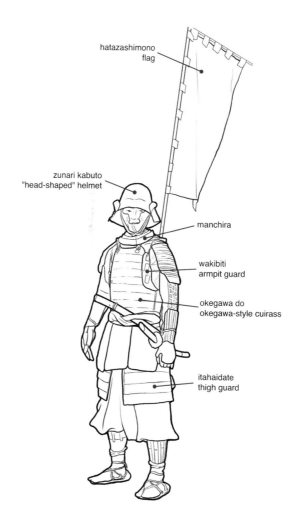

hatazashimono flag

zunari kabuto "head-shaped" helmet

manchira

wakibiti armpit guard

okegawa do okegawa-style cuirass

itahaidate thigh guard

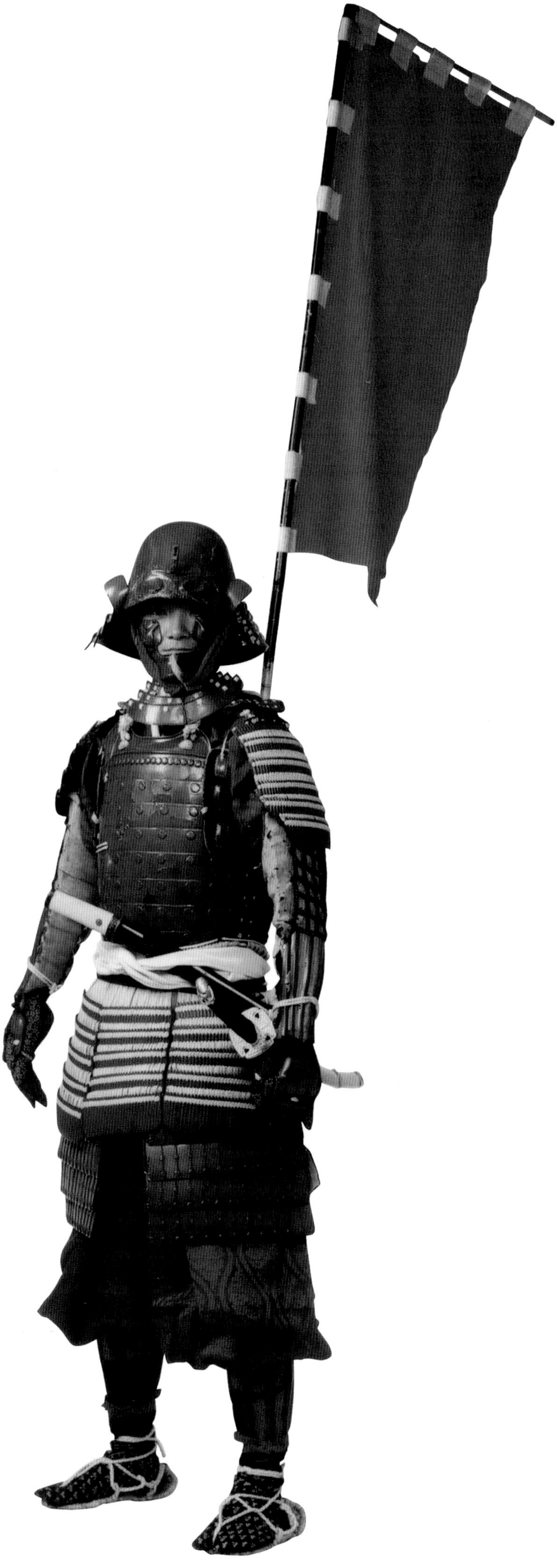

Overall, the red-lacquered armor is of okegawado style, fasted together and retained in place with cord.

About a hundred years after the era of the renowned Naomasa, the camp of what remained of the once glorious "red forces" of Ii came under night attack by a much more modern army made up of the commoners of Choshu.

The Ii army fled from the camp, leaving behind all of their belongings, including their famous red armor. This was then returned to its owners by the Choshu folk as symbol of the disgrace of the noble Ii clan.

Left: Ii Naomasa's banner was always a red flag (here shown without his personal character sign), to match the color of his armor. It would have been carried at the rear in the usual gattari flagpole attachment.

Above: *Seen up close, the red-lacquered helmet shows clear signs of wear, with bare metal visible at the front edge by the decorative device. The molded face guard was used to fix the chinstrap and helmet cords.*

Right: *Detailed view of the whole cuirass, lacquered in red with cross-shaped braiding cord resembling metal bolts. There is also a rare type of upper arm protector and the hilt of the dagger is expensively covered with sharkskin.*

GOMAIDO ARMOR
Sengoku period

The famous samurai warlord "One-eyed Jack", Date Masamune (1566-1636), in his domaru armor and jinbaori surcoat. The eye patch on his right injured eye was made from a piece of sword guard. In wearing the jinbaori, he has left off the sode shoulder guard, although he has lower leg protection made of metal plate.

The helmet was made of sixteen triangular pieces of iron with a central hole on top decorated with brass metal. Although the hole provided good ventilation, it was actually what was left after the adaptation of the older style of bolted helmet. Inside, its cloth lining is stitched spirally to make it hemispherical in shape.

The okegawado style of armor included a cuirass made of transverse plates, but gomaido armor, as seen here, consisted of vertical plates with an inside covered with leather.

Since this type of armor, or *gomaido-tatehagi-hotokedo*, was specially produced at Yukinoshita in Kamakura, it was often called *youkinoshitado*.

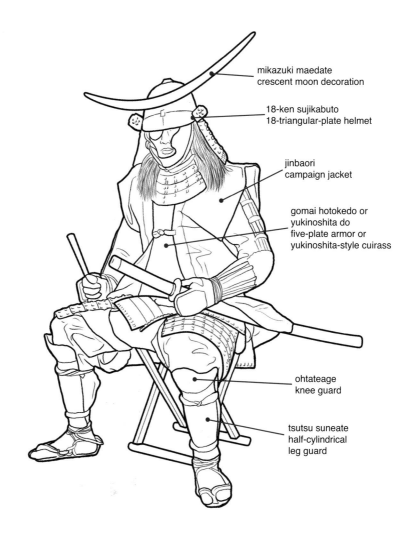

mikazuki maedate
crescent moon decoration

18-ken sujikabuto
18-triangular-plate helmet

jinbaori
campaign jacket

gomai hotokedo or
yukinoshita do
five-plate armor or
yukinoshita-style cuirass

ohtateage
knee guard

tsutsu suneate
half-cylindrical
leg guard

Date Masamune greatly favored the amor's style and so it was also adopted by his retainers. Even later, it was even also called *sendai-do* armor, in honor of Masamune's domain.

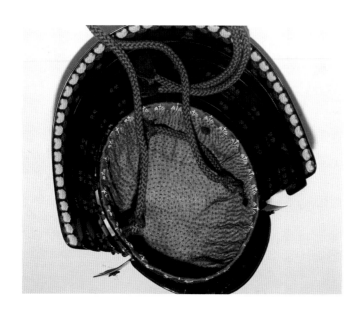

Above: *In the fine surcoat, the warlord with his hair-knot untied under the helmet, a practice that emerged during the mid-Kamakura period. His helmet also identifies him specifically as Date Masamune as it carries the large sickle-shaped decoration that was the one-eyed warlord's personal motif.*

Left: *Inside and outside detail views of the helmet, showing the brass-ringed ventilation hole at the top and the spirally stitched inner lining.*

Right: The okegawado style of armor cuirass in close-up and showing its construction as being of vertical plates.

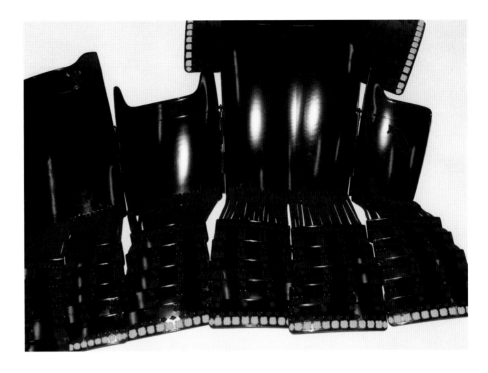

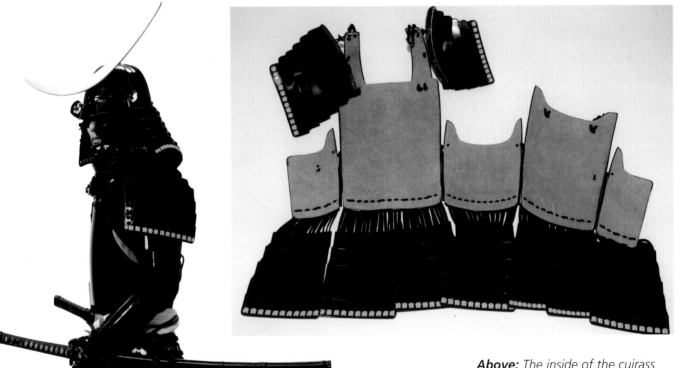

Above: The inside of the cuirass with its leather coverings.

Left: Side view from the left showing the armor as worn with the shoulder guard. The style usually incorporated the jinbaori with a lower side vent for the sword. However, in this case, there is clearly no vent.

KARTASANE PLATE ARMOR
Late Sengoku to Edo period

Even by this time, not all armor was made to all the latest adopted styles. However, in the Nara period, the then government adopted what was a Chinese-style of armor supposedly similar to the newest designs of the time. Alas, there are no surviving examples of these Nara-period outfits. Nevertheless, from the Chinese armor of that time, it seems reasonable to speculate that the Japanese equivalent also used rectangular plates sewn onto padded cloth.

Certainly, plate-style armor seemed to disappear from the scene for a while, consistent with the lack of any surviving Nara-period examples. Later, though, by the Muromachi period, there are once more surviving descriptions of plate style armor.

In fact, it was relatively easy to produce the small iron plates than the much longer plates for other styles of armor. The small rectangular plates were then interconnected by chain mail and sewn onto the underlining cloth to crate the garments.

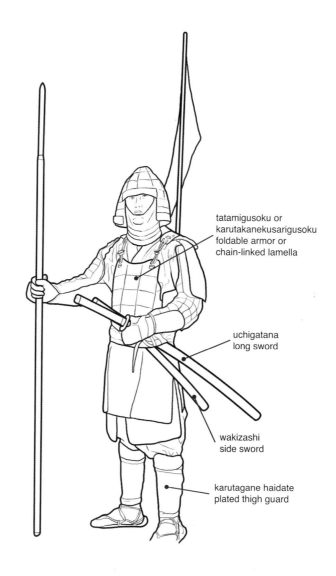

tatamigusoku or karutakanekusarigusoku foldable armor or chain-linked lamella

uchigatana long sword

wakizashi side sword

karutagane haidate plated thigh guard

This is authentic, antique kartazane armor that had become much lighter to wear without the heavier metal cuirass, he is armed with a pair of swords as well as a long spear.

On the complete suit of kartasane armor it is evident that the construction of its chain mail is different from that used in Europe and consists of interconnecting circular and oval metal rings. The helmet is made form a series of metal plates although its connecting rings appear to have become partially broken over the years.

Armor of this type had one overriding advantage in that it was easy to pack. When a warlord needed to mobilize his huge forces, it became necessary to transport a huge collection of cases and boxes of armor. But the kartazane outfit was easy to fold and several sets could be packed in a single container/ Consequently, when Toyotomi Hideyoshi invaded Korea in 1592, kartazane armor proved especially convenient to transport by ship.

Above: *Seen from the rear, it is apparent that this armor style no longer included a flagpole container although there are still upper and lower bottom supports. For the purpose of the photographic session of this well-preserved armor, a flag was actually pushed into the back of the obi, something that would not really have happened at the time. Prominent too is the shoulder guard, under which the cloth was covered with small hexagonal metal plates tied by violet cord. It was called a manchira, a name that derived from the Dutch word "mantel."*

Left: *Close-up of the helmet showing its sectioned construction, cheek, and neck guards. The shoulder straps and cuirass fastenings are also evident.*

Above: The plate construction of the cuirass can be clearly seen along with a neck guard of chain mail.

Left: Without spear or lance and in charging mode, a running samurai always carried his sword in this way, on the right shoulder. Not only was this safer when encountering an ally, it was just as convenient in enabling the fighter to make the quick first blow to the enemy.

GUNNER'S MOGAMIDO ARMOR
Sengoku period

Mogamido armor consisted of six large front and rear metal plates, and four narrow side plates. In turn, each plate was made up of seven rows of even smaller metal plates, each row connected by tied cords.

The samurai gun was a short arquebus of large caliber. The gunner's helmet is of the *zunarikabuto* ("head shaped") style with the sikoro covered in yak hair. It also carries a large decorative circular maedate called *wanuki*.

Awaiting the approaching enemy, the gunner wound the smoldering fuse cord around his wrist, blowing upon on it in order to keep it alight. Then, there was a definite sequence of drill for loading and firing the arquebus.

If fired from a standing position, gunpowder was first poured into the muzzle, followed by the bullet or ball and the muzzle tamped down hard and deep with a ramrod. Additional powder was then added to the fireplate and its cover closed to prevent a premature blast. The glowing fuse cord was then attached to the lock and the weapon aimed. Opening the plate cover gently, the gun was then fired.

After only a few firings, a build-up of ash restricted the muzzle diameter considerably and smaller caliber shot had to be used. Alternatively, if the gunner had a spare

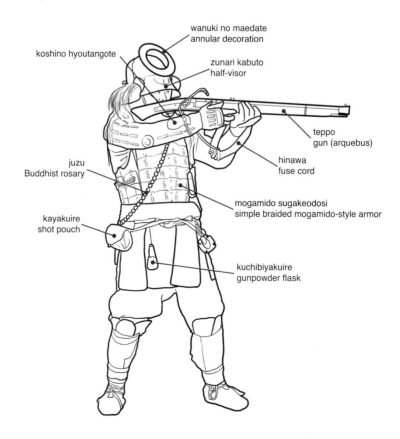

wanuki no maedate
annular decoration

koshino hyoutangote

zunari kabuto
half-visor

juzu
Buddhist rosary

teppo
gun (arquebus)

hinawa
fuse cord

mogamido sugakeodosi
simple braided mogamido-style armor

kayakuire
shot pouch

kuchibiyakuire
gunpowder flask

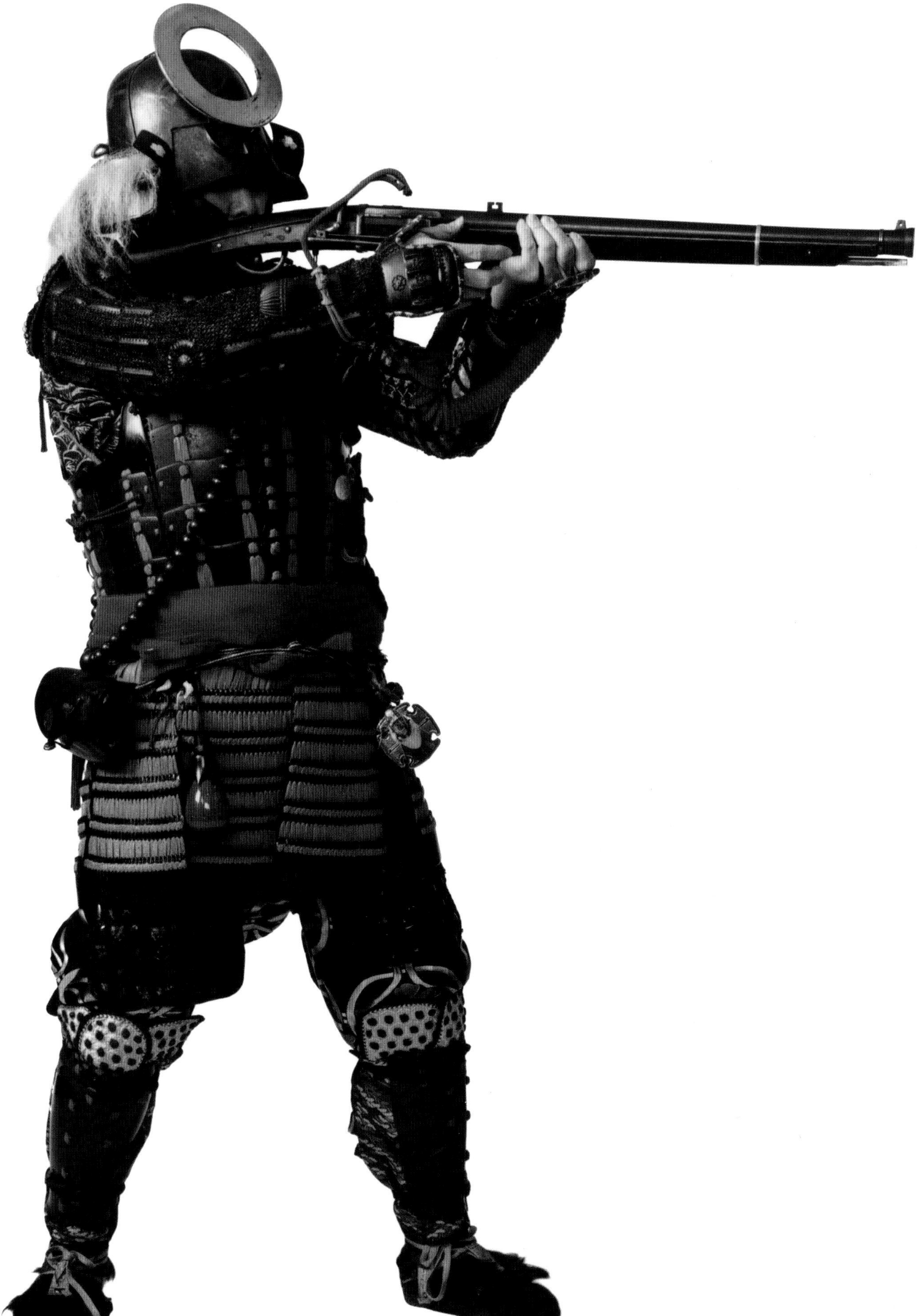

weapon, he would change guns and hand the discharged one to his retainer.

The latter would then quickly dismantle the barrel and stock, dislodge the rear screw, clean the barrel and refit the the parts ready for the gunner's next shot.

Below: *Detailed view of the front of the armor showing the plates and sugakeodosi straight braiding, which can be seen under a large Buddhist rosary that the gunner is also wearing.*

Above: *At the rear of the armor, which has here been replaced with chain mail in order to reduce weight and provide ventilation, there is the usual flagpole socket. With the additional view of the shoulder guard also of a chain mail, its method of manufacture is very clear.*

Above: The first part of the well-defined sequence of loading and firing was the charging of the weapon with gunpowder before introducing the ammunition down the muzzle.

Right: Carried in the usual rear-mounted flag carrier, the gunner wears his force's insignia device. On his helmet is a variation of the many designs that were favored, this being made of wood and covered with gold foil.

NANBANDO "SOUTHERN BARBARIAN" ARMOR
Sengoku to early Edo period

The word *nanbanjin*, meaning "southern barbarian", referred to any people who came to Japan from the "south". However, it did not necessarily mean that the Japanese of the period considered all foreigners to be barbarians and was simply another way of saying, in effect, "stranger from the south" Thus, the term included the Portuguese, Spanish, Dutch and, later, the British, the USA having not yet appeared on the scene.

This heavily-armed arquebus gunner is in true antique armor and carries a large golden insignia on his back. The short, large-caliber gun was used mainly used by samurai sharpshooters, while a long and small caliber type was used by ashigaru.

Deliberate pockmarks were included in the armor's manufacture in order to indicate that it was bullet proof. It was also a sign that the armor might not be of Spanish origin but, rather, that it was made in Japan.

The gunner carries the fuse cord on his right wrist but still wears a sword and in the tachi way.

The striking circular insignia was made of

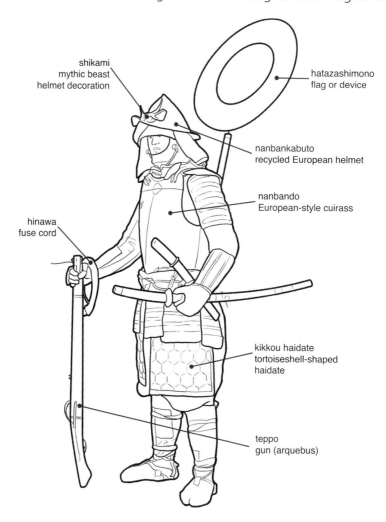

shikami
mythic beast
helmet decoration

hatazashimono
flag or device

nanbankabuto
recycled European helmet

nanbando
European-style cuirass

hinawa
fuse cord

kikkou haidate
tortoiseshell-shaped
haidate

teppo
gun (arquebus)

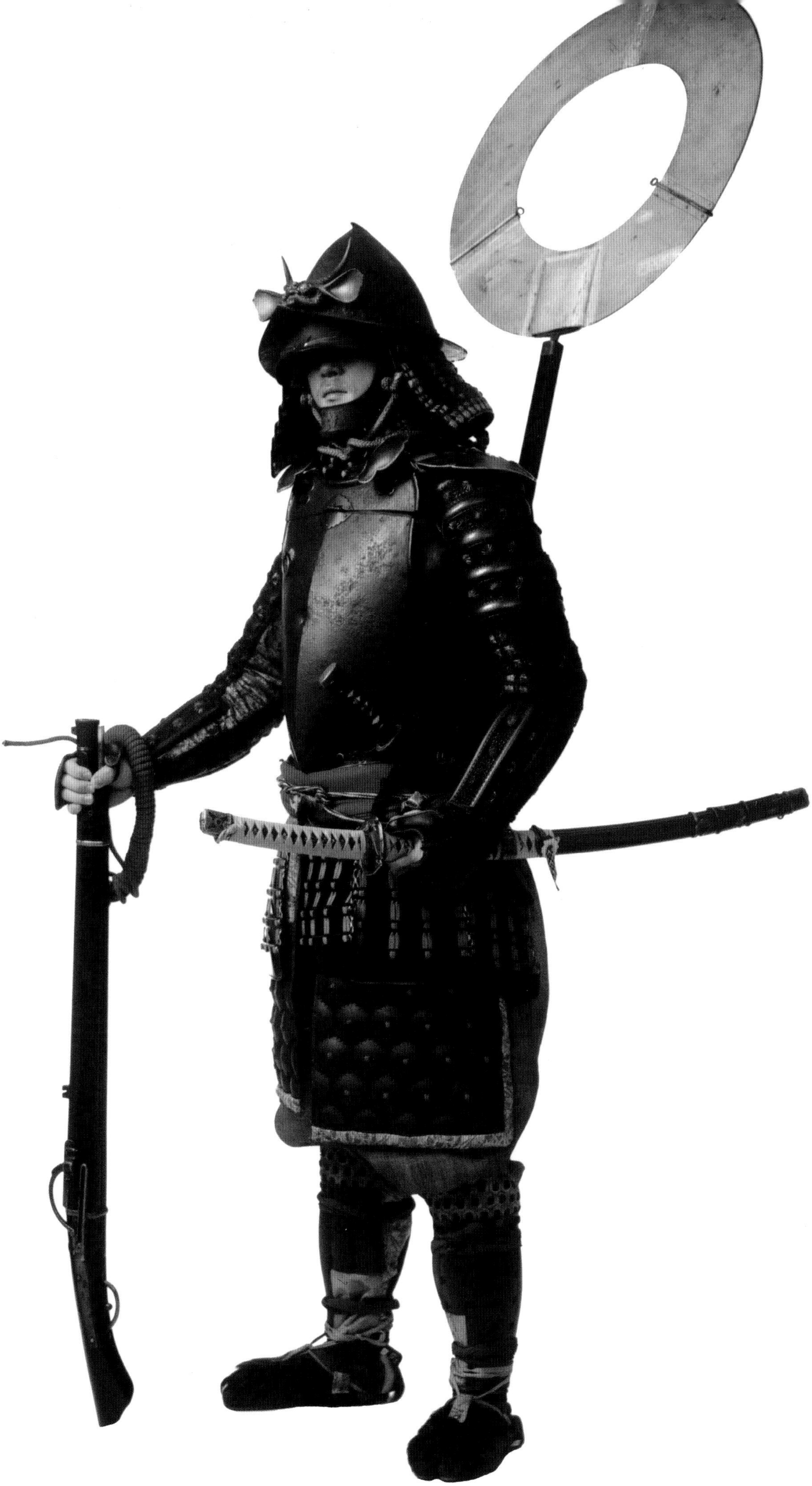

wood and coated with gold leaf. It was made up of three parts.

In appearance, the gunner's helmet looks like as if traditional *zunari* has been covered by Spanish helmet, or that the top of the zunari helmet was removed and attached to Spanish cabasset. Whichever, it carries the traditional and favorite shikami decoration and has hanpo half-cheek type guards. At its rear, the kusazuri neck guard is more traditional in form.

The cuirass, however, also shows distinct Spanish or Portuguese influences, although of probable Japanese origin. Its upper body has been modified and a new part was fitted; the small brass ring on the chest is a staff holder. At the rear of the cuirass would have been a wooden gattari flag holder.

More foreign influence is evident in the fact of the shoulder guard looking rather non-Japanese in style. The kote gauntlets too are unusual as the half-ring-shaped upper arm guard was rarely attached in this traverse way, especially if the kote were originally attached to the armor.

The thigh guard consists of hexagonal plates are connected by ring mail and the overall impression here is one of nanbando armor being downright heavy. Indeed, to a modern eye, doing battle in such an outfit, especially in summer heat, looks as if it would have been extremely tiring, other than for a few minutes. Only high-class samurai or a commander is likely to have actually preferred such bulletproof but heavy protection.

Above: *Ready for battle with the dented cuirass, gun, fuse cord and sword, with the gold-leaf insignia being worn and carried at the rear in the usual gattari holder.*

Left: *Detail of the foreign-influenced shoulder guard and the front of the cuirass with its brass ring for holding a staff*

Left: *Detailed view of the helmet with its traditional horned shikami device attached to what is probably an adapted Spanish helmet. The cheek guard and upper face guard are clearly visible along with the fixing cords. Such helmet decorations—like flag symbols—indicated the wearer's religious views, such as his worship of the sun, moon, Devil, or Buddha. However, some symbols were also of a somewhat insulting or satirical nature towards the enemy, such as the belittling message of the haetori ("catching a fly").*

Below: *A closer look at the heavily protective arm guards and gauntlets; doubtless effective against gunfire but probably heavy to use in a sword fight.*

Below: *Rear detail of the adapted helmet but with the traditional neck guard in place.*

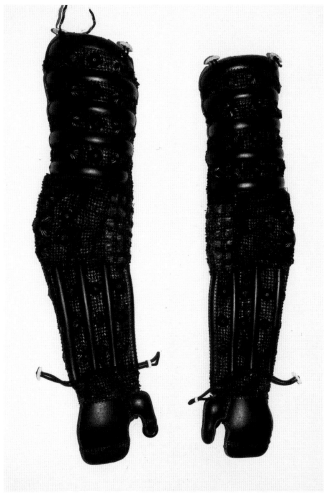

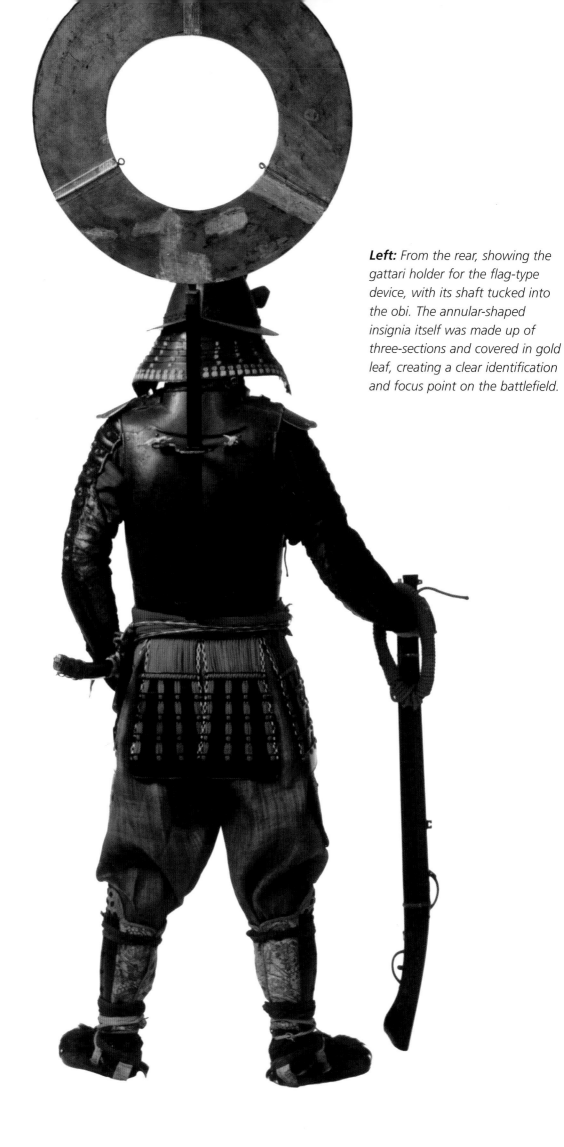

Left: *From the rear, showing the gattari holder for the flag-type device, with its shaft tucked into the obi. The annular-shaped insignia itself was made up of three-sections and covered in gold leaf, creating a clear identification and focus point on the battlefield.*

Left: Close-up of the thigh guard showing the hexagonal plates and additional decoration.

Below: The foreign-influenced cuirass in detail, with attached guard panels and a modified upper part and the (probably deliberate) dents of battle or gun fire.

KATAGINU AND HAKAMA (KAMISHIMO)
Edo period

Differing from the older style of kataginu seen earlier in these pages, the front hangings were by then folded into the hakama in parallel folds. As explained previously, the kataginu had evolved from the suho by removing the latter's large sleeves for convenience.

However, this newer style, once adopted as formal dress and give its wear a more dignified air, extended the line of the shoulder again. In addition, the previously-shortened hakama gained extra length and so lost any functionality other than for the ceremonial occasions. Rather than wanting the practicality of Sengoku clothing, samurai began to behave dress in manners similar to peacetime bureaucrats.

For formal official dress, the samurai wore the kataginu and hakama over of a kosode.

However, the eboshi cap was only worn at important formal ceremonies in the shogun's office and over a top hair-knot that is typical of the Edo period.

When the kataginu and hakama were of a matching color, it had the specific name of *kami-shimo* or "top and bottom".

In his daily duty of office, not even a samurai was now allowed to wear a sword.

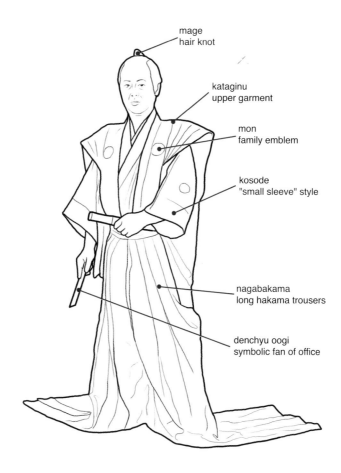

mage
hair knot

kataginu
upper garment

mon
family emblem

kosode
"small sleeve" style

nagabakama
long hakama trousers

denchyu oogi
symbolic fan of office

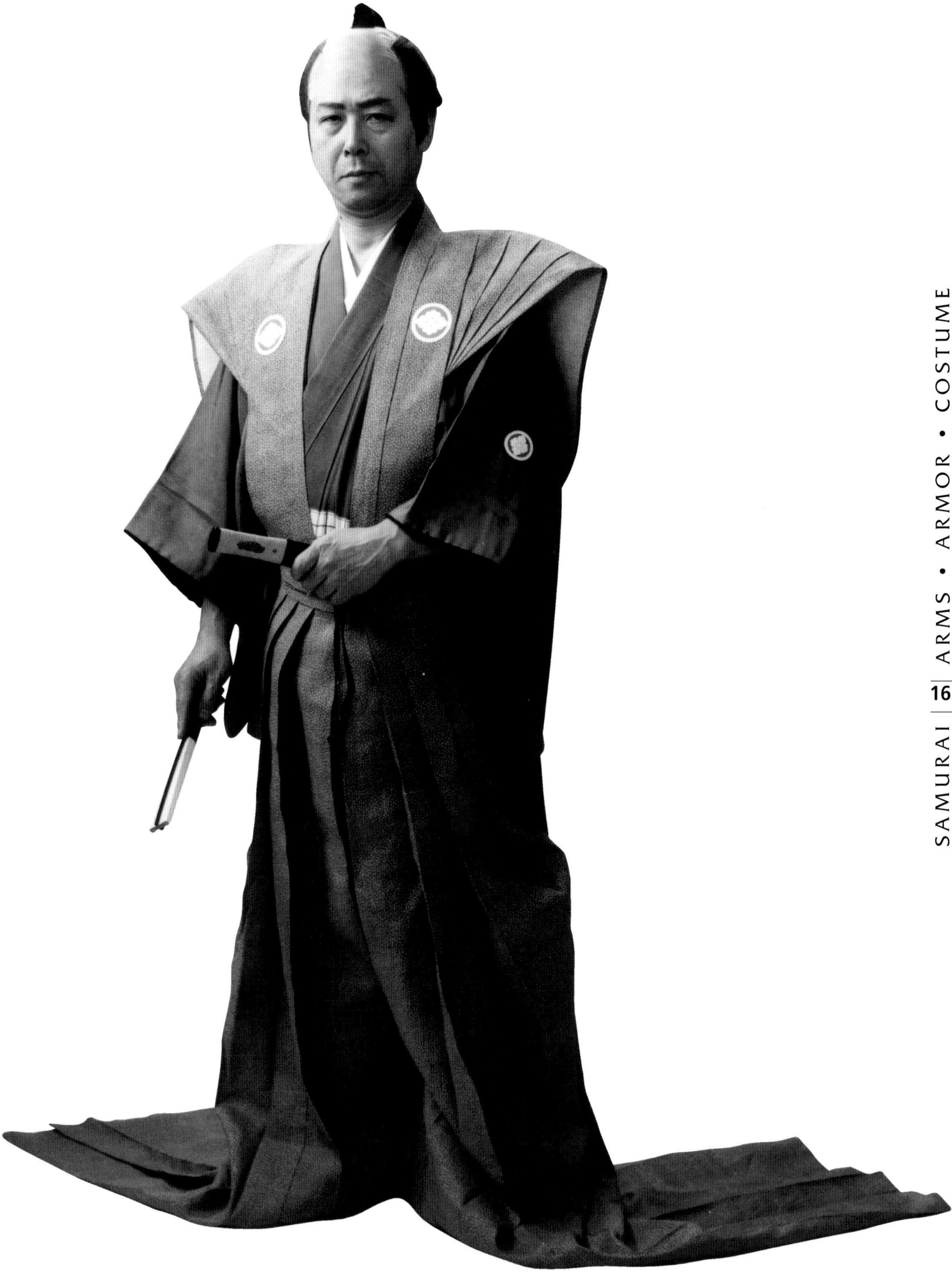

Right: *By this time not even a samurai was allowed to carry a sword when in office. Instead, he tended to wear a small knife or dagger tucked into his obi belt, as seen here.*

Left: *Although considered formal wear, the kataginu would still incorporate the wearer's family emblem as can be seen in this rear view, where the crest is featured on the back of the hakama.*

Left and below: *Reverentially kneeling before becoming seated for a formal meeting with the shogun. During the Edo period, the government forbad the growing of facial hair such as a beard or moustache, and so the samurai wears no eboshi cap and his futatsuori-mage or folded hair-knot is clearly visible on a partially shaved head. However, he still carries his dagger.*

effective against an enemy not wearing armor. It was very much something for a more direct, one-to-one situation where such rapid action might save one's life. But in the more peaceful times, could one be so sure that the person you just killed had indeed been an enemy and of murderous intent?

Even in peacetime, the spear did not lost its function as defensive weapon, especially if attacked at home by an intruder. In such circumstances, it proved itself to be really useful, since sword fighting in typical small, low-roofed room was rather inconvenient, to say the least.

Right: *The "quick draw'" deployment of the sword was one that evolved in this period and used when the samurai felt threatened or was actually under attack.*

Above: It might have been a time of peace, but if threatened at home by an intruder, the samurai could still use his yari spear as a more effective weapon for use indoors. So, protected on his left side he holds the spear head-down with a raised right hand, with the left hand acting as a fulcrum. The right hand would then have been pushed forward towards the attacker's face.

Right: When walking out, wearing a haori over his kosode and hakama, the samurai still remained a formidable figure, with sword, dagger, and fan of office, all tucked into an obi belt. The haori carries his family crest at the front, just below the shoulders.

FIRE-FIGHTING OUTFIT
Edo period

A population census carried out from 1716 to 1736 by the Tokugawa bakufu revealed that the population in Edo was around a million, making it (at the time and in as far as comparative numbers from elsewhere were known or accurate) the world's largest city.

Earlier, in 1657, a huge fire had occurred in Edo, burning down most of the city and resulting in some 100,000 fatalities.

After the fire, the Tokugawa bakufu samurai government restored Edo with new concepts such as broadening the roads, establishing adequate water reservoirs, establishing an organized fire brigade, and so forth.

The fire brigade was called the called the *jobikeshi*, and its four leaders (they later became ten) were appointed from the old shogun guard. However, in addition to the jobikeshi, warlords resident in Edo city also set up their own body of fire-fighters.

Just like the bakufu, their concern was that In winter, the strong dry wind in Edo often contributed to a spate of big fires that were regarded by its citizens as being both spectacular in effect but also disastrous in outcome.

In fact, it has been said that fire and fighting were the very hallmarks of Edo city. Unlike the daimyo firefighters, the machibikeshi citizens brigade were as apt to fight amongst themselves when on duty as to fight any fire. Thus, for onlookers, there

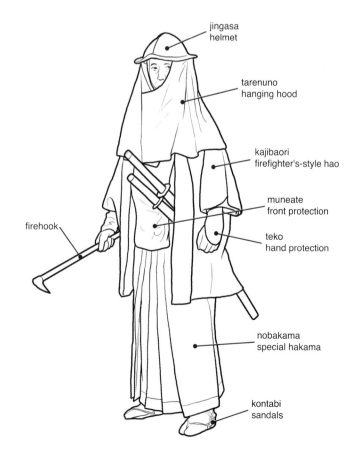

jingasa
helmet

tarenuno
hanging hood

kajibaori
firefighter's-style hao

muneate
front protection

teko
hand protection

firehook

nobakama
special hakama

kontabi
sandals

were often the simultaneous and twin spectacles of conflict and conflagration!

The daimyo hikeshi warlord fire-fighter depicted here is wearing a *jingasa* helmet with a cloth hood.

With the hood open, he carries his fire hook as a staff, indicating is position as a jobikeshi leader.

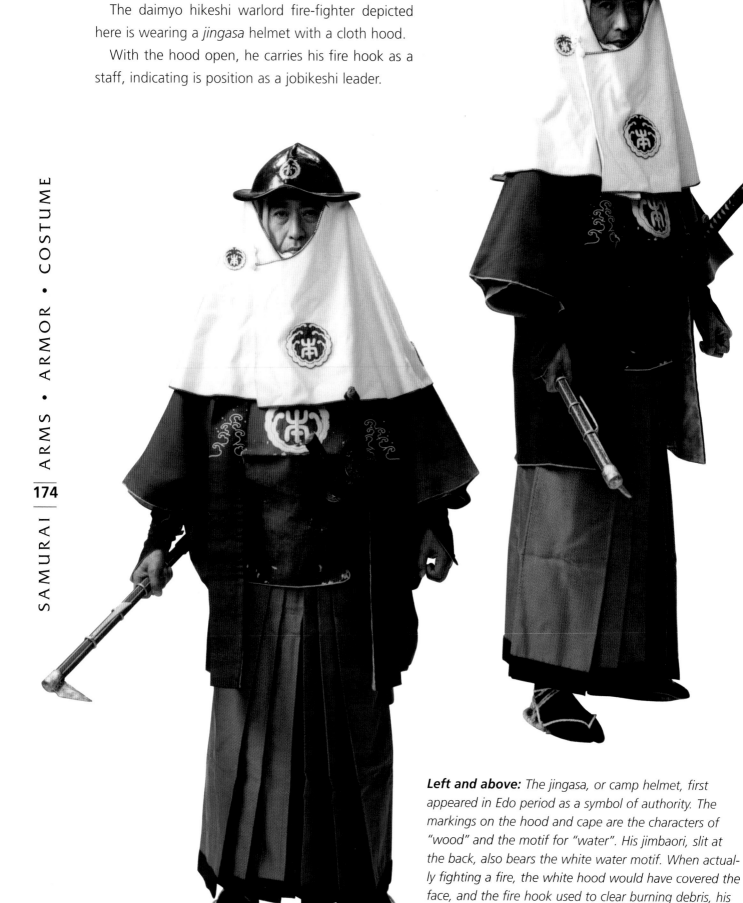

Left and above: *The jingasa, or camp helmet, first appeared in Edo period as a symbol of authority. The markings on the hood and cape are the characters of "wood" and the motif for "water". His jimbaori, slit at the back, also bears the white water motif. When actually fighting a fire, the white hood would have covered the face, and the fire hook used to clear burning debris, his two swords being for self-defense.*

Left: From the rear, one can see that the jimbaori, slit at the back, also bears the white water motif and in "reversed" colors on the rear of the protective hood.

NANBANDO ARMOR WITH SAIKA HELMET

Early Edo period

The effect upon on the Japanese armor industry of external Spanish influence was very productive and innovative. Although the samurai who actually fought in battle did not want to wear such heavy protection, their commanders actively sought out hardened metal armor.

At first, armorers simply adopted and adapted actual Spanish armor. However, they soon began to produce their own versions, albeit similar in style, but with a dimpled front that was a result of testing that the cuirass was indeed bulletproof.

The seated samurai commander in the nanbando wears a rear-mounted red flag.

The top grade helmet style is of a special kind called saikahati . It was named this way in honor of the town of Saika in Kishu (Wakayama) province that was famous for producing high quality iron.

His cuirass is embossed with a character meaning "to flow" and the haidate thigh protector is made up of a series of narrow iron plates.

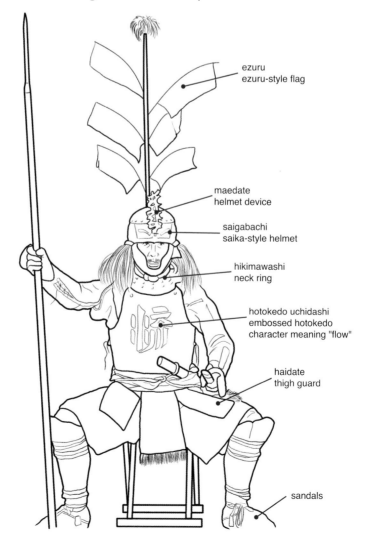

ezuru
ezuru-style flag

maedate
helmet device

saigabachi
saika-style helmet

hikimawashi
neck ring

hotokedo uchidashi
embossed hotokedo
character meaning "flow"

haidate
thigh guard

sandals

Above: *Although armed with a fine sword, the spear or lance remained a favorite weapon. The shoes would have been covered with bearskin.*

Left: *The "sectioned" design of the rear-worn flag device was intended to lessen the effect of any strong wind on the battlefield.*

Right: A close-up look at the kusazuri, showing its lower half covered by bearskin to match the shoes.

Below: Detailed view of the saika-hati iron helmet showing its lamel-lae structure and the sikoro's yak hair covering and the brass motif representing a section from a Sanskrit-based Buddhist chant.

RAIDING OUTFIT
Edo period

In peacetime, although the samurai were no longer busy killing each other (as is described in many of the previous pages), they were often still inclined to solve a problem by force. Revenge for any real or perceived wrongs to family or a relative was officially sanctioned by the Edo government. Indeed, it was felt to be a duty, rather being obligatory, such that that an avenging samurai might pursue and seek out a runaway enemy for several years.

It was regarded by the warrior as an honorable quest as much as anything, for there was no guarantee of a victorious revenge, even if he were luckily to find the enemy. Such gallant ventures produced many a tragic story.

Ready to fight, the samurai is wearing hachimaki headgear that has been reinforced with a metal plate.

The right sleeve of his kosode has been removed and chain mail has been sewn into a blue undershirt and metal plates were even hidden within the blue gloves and revealed by their brown rust stains

The sword was drawn from the scabbard by turning the right hand in a circular motion that was necessitated by the long blade.

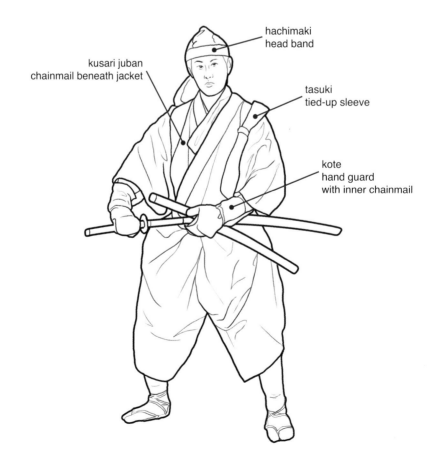

hachimaki
head band

kusari juban
chainmail beneath jacket

tasuki
tied-up sleeve

kote
hand guard
with inner chainmail

Above and right: *The sword, drawn from the scabbard with a right-handed circular motion, is now raised in attack mode, either as a threat or to inflict real damage to an enemy.*

Right: Seen from the rear and showing how the white cloth belt was fastened to the hanging sleeves, and crosses the raider's back, whilst the long hachimaki hangs over the left shoulder.

CITY MAGISTRATE
Edo period

By this time, a samurai never walked with woman in public. Indeed, it was prohibited to do so, a custom and practice that was derived from one of the tenets of Confucianism that gave men the dominance over women.

Confucianism, although Chinese in origin, was adopted by the Tokugawa bakufu as a supreme ideology and was inherent in maintaining the samurai regime and ethos. The modern samurai code is one of peacetime and dates from the Edo period itself.

The struggle at that time was, therefore, very against the previous ideology that existed during centuries of war. The bakufu adoption of Confucianism we thus a shrewd and (maybe) opportunistic move at the time.

There were two police departments in Edo city, north and south. Here, a *yoriki* chief inspector on duty wears the distinctive helmet that was specially developed in Edo period. Using it as a staff, he is holding a *jutte* ("ten hands"), a type of truncheon that was is used in the arrest of criminals and the tassel color of which was defined by the officer's rank.

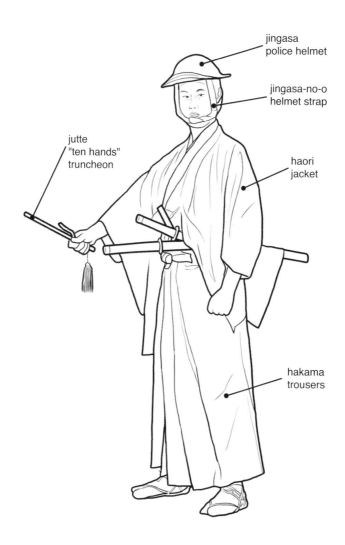

jingasa
police helmet

jingasa-no-o
helmet strap

jutte
"ten hands"
truncheon

haori
jacket

hakama
trousers

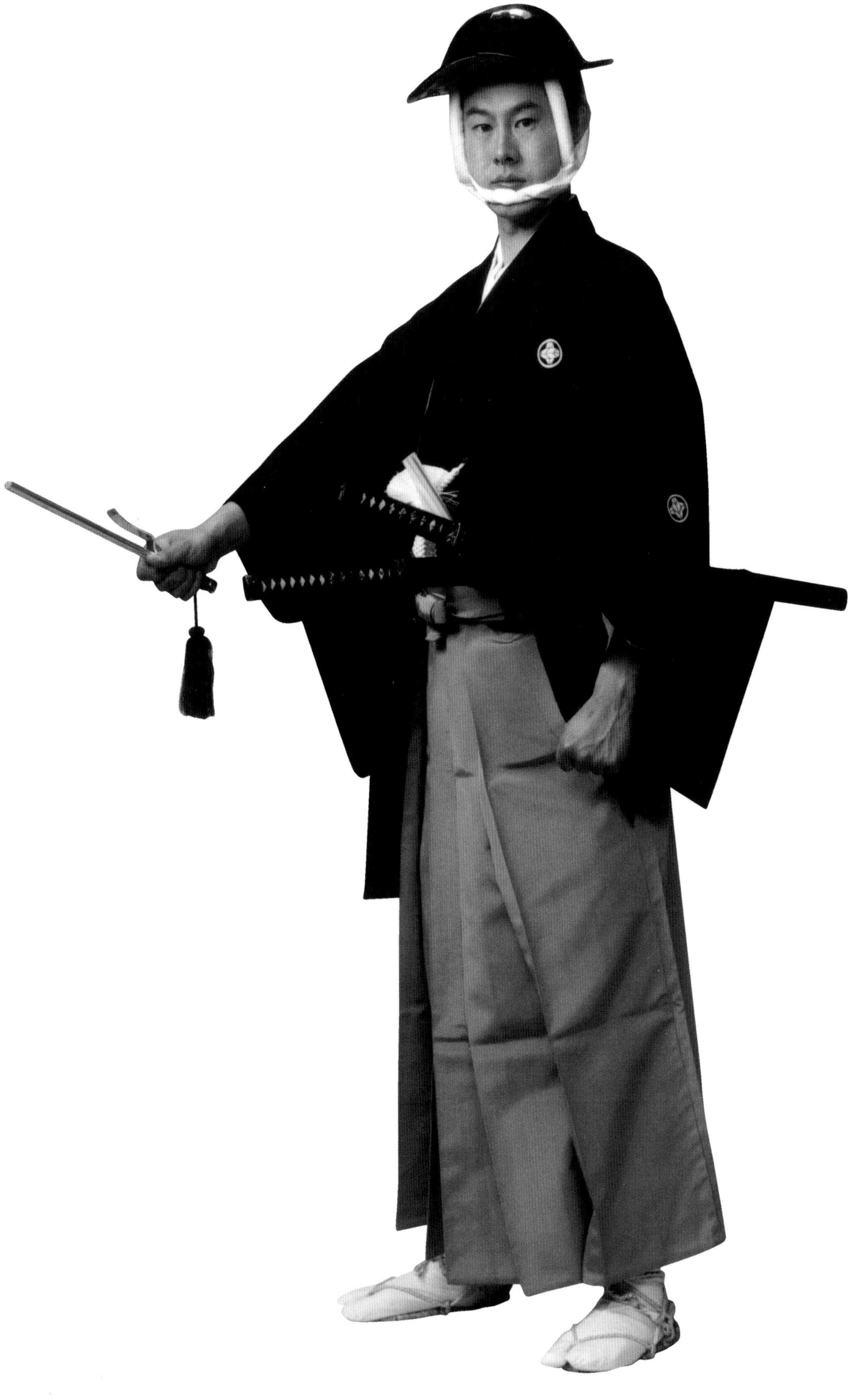

Right: Even when not on duty, helmet-less and with his hair-knot visible, the yoriki chief inspector is ready to draw his sword if necessary.

Left: On duty, wearing the special helmet, sword, dagger, and carrying the "ten hands" jutte.

Despite the Edo-period social convention of not being able stroll out with a female companion, even his wife, it was permissible for a samurai to walk in his own garden dressed in this type of informal outfit that includes a haori, hakama and a sword worn horizontally (unlike the ronin style of the time).

DOSHIN POLICE
Late Edo period

The ashigaru class was mobilized for police duty and was on constant patrol in the city of Edo. In order to gain information and maintain their intelligence on the criminal fraternity, they needed to keep in close contact with the civilian population.

Those doshin who were attached to the two magistrate offices in Edo city were regarded as being particularly up-to-date I their style. This officer is even wearing woman's kosode and the lower half of the haori is folded in the obi belt for easier movement. Wearing a woman's kosode was very much "the thing" of the time and was adopted by the trendsetters and playboys of the Edo period, and consequently was copied by the doshin

The doshin and their activities have provided a good source of stories and background for modern TV and movies depicting the late Edo period.

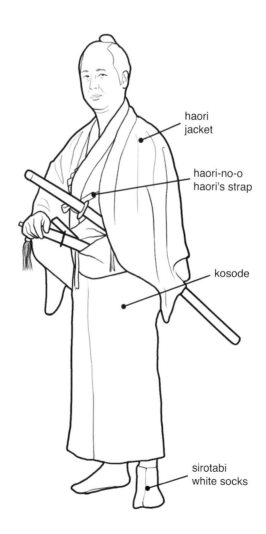

haori
jacket

haori-no-o
haori's strap

kosode

sirotabi
white socks

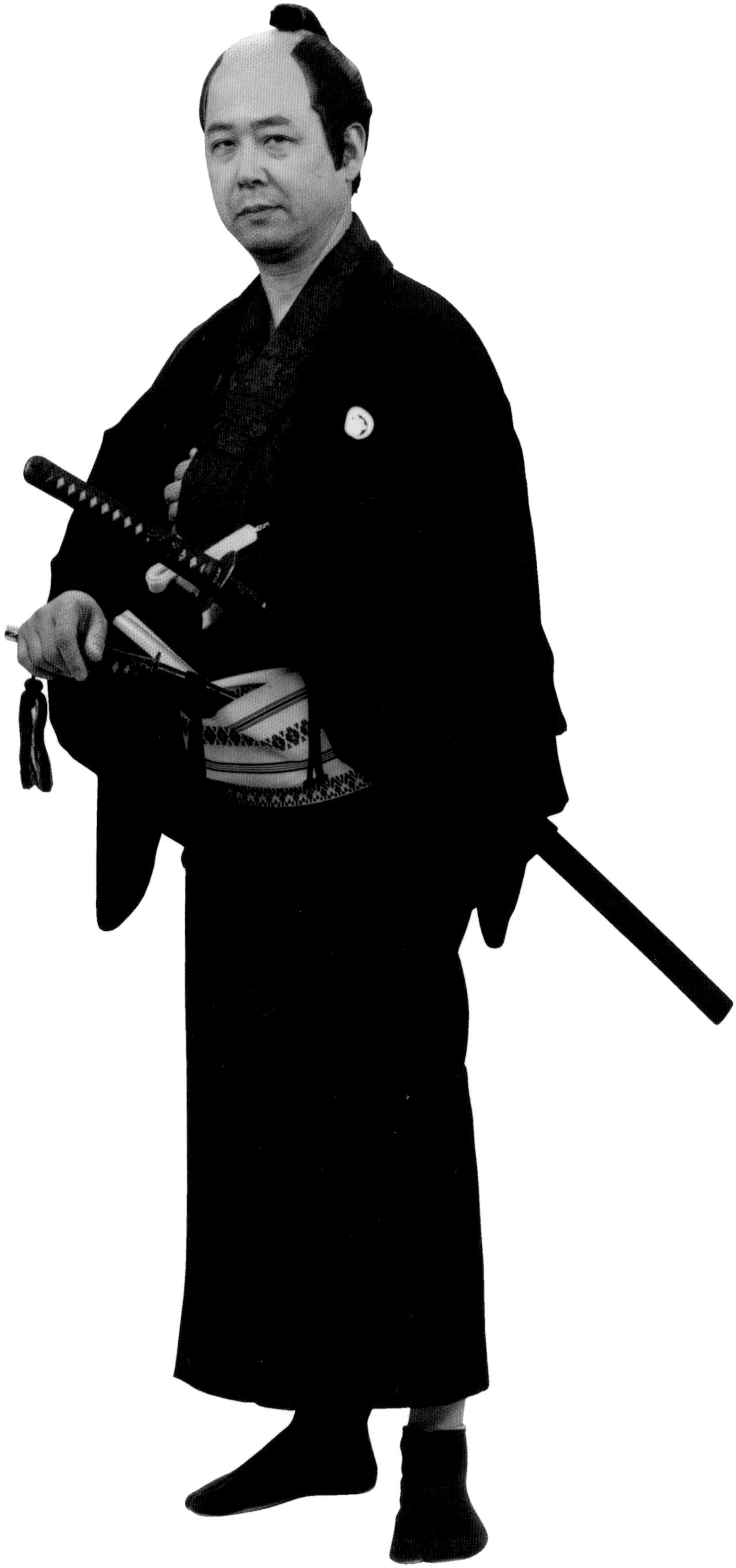

Right: *In a sequence that might even be a modern TV or movie depiction of the doshin, it is nevertheless true that skilled use of the jutte would often protect an officer from an assassin's hand.*

Below: *Goyoda! ("You are under arrest").*

Left: *The doshin places his left arm inside the kosode, removing it from the sleeve and resting his hand on the jutte tucked into the obi. As intimated, in modern reconstructions, all of this may represent a degree of artistic license. In reality, the officer would have carried his jutte inside the kosode, so that it was never visible from the outside.*

LADY'S CLASSIC COSTUME
Edo period

The kosode style emerged in the late Azuchi-Momoyama period. In its female form, it was once basically underwear that had evolved into being women's formal dress in the Edo period. Its name is probably the basic word from which evolved the modern term "kimono".

The obi is fastened on her back and her distinctive hairstyle, which developed in this period. In fact, it is the forerunner of the modern style that is often still worn by a modern Japanese bride at her wedding, albeit usually in the form of a wig.

However, in the Edo times, if married, she would also have shaved her eyebrows and painted her teeth black, although the latter practice is scarcely ever shown today in TV, movie or drama representations of the period.

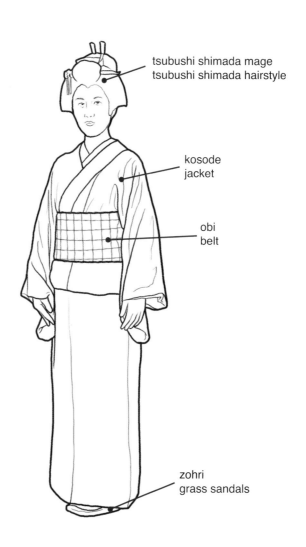

tsubushi shimada mage
tsubushi shimada hairstyle

kosode
jacket

obi
belt

zohri
grass sandals

Left: *The costume as seen from the rear and showing the fastening method of the broad obi.*

Right: *Unlike the prevailing style of the Azuchi-momoyama period, ladies could now sit holding both of her knees in the full, male samurai-style.*

Right: When out walking, a lady of the Edo period would have worn a hood like this in order not to show too much of her face.

SPECIAL-DUTY POLICE
Late Edo period

The Edo bakufu ruled over Japan peacefully for some 250 years. However, the world outside was changing and hitherto isolated Japan was shaken by the increased colonialism of Western nations. Britain, France, Russia and USA pressurized the Tokugawa bakufu forcefully to open Japan for trade and ever more contact.

Finally, the bakufu decided to open some harbors to foreign ships foreign countries. But the Komei emperor in Kyto disliked foreigners and his aristocrat followers remained largely ignorant of the great changes taking place elsewhere in the world.

The most radical elements even tried to abolish the samurai government when the Tokugawa bakufu admitted too accepting the arrival of overseas vessel in some Japanese ports. Samurai who were against bakufu policies and decisions in this context began a campaign of outright terrorism not only opposing Tokugawa samurai but any intellectuals, merchants or police

In order to try to counter the terrorism, the bakufu organized the formation and deployment of "special-duty" police in Kyoto. These consisted of two different organizations, the Mimawarigumi and the Shinsengumi.

The former consisted of sons of old guard and the latter of volunteers from Kanto area.

The counter-terrorist group was organized by order of the Tokugawa

haori
jacket

uwaobi
belt

kote
arm and hand guard

hakama
trousers

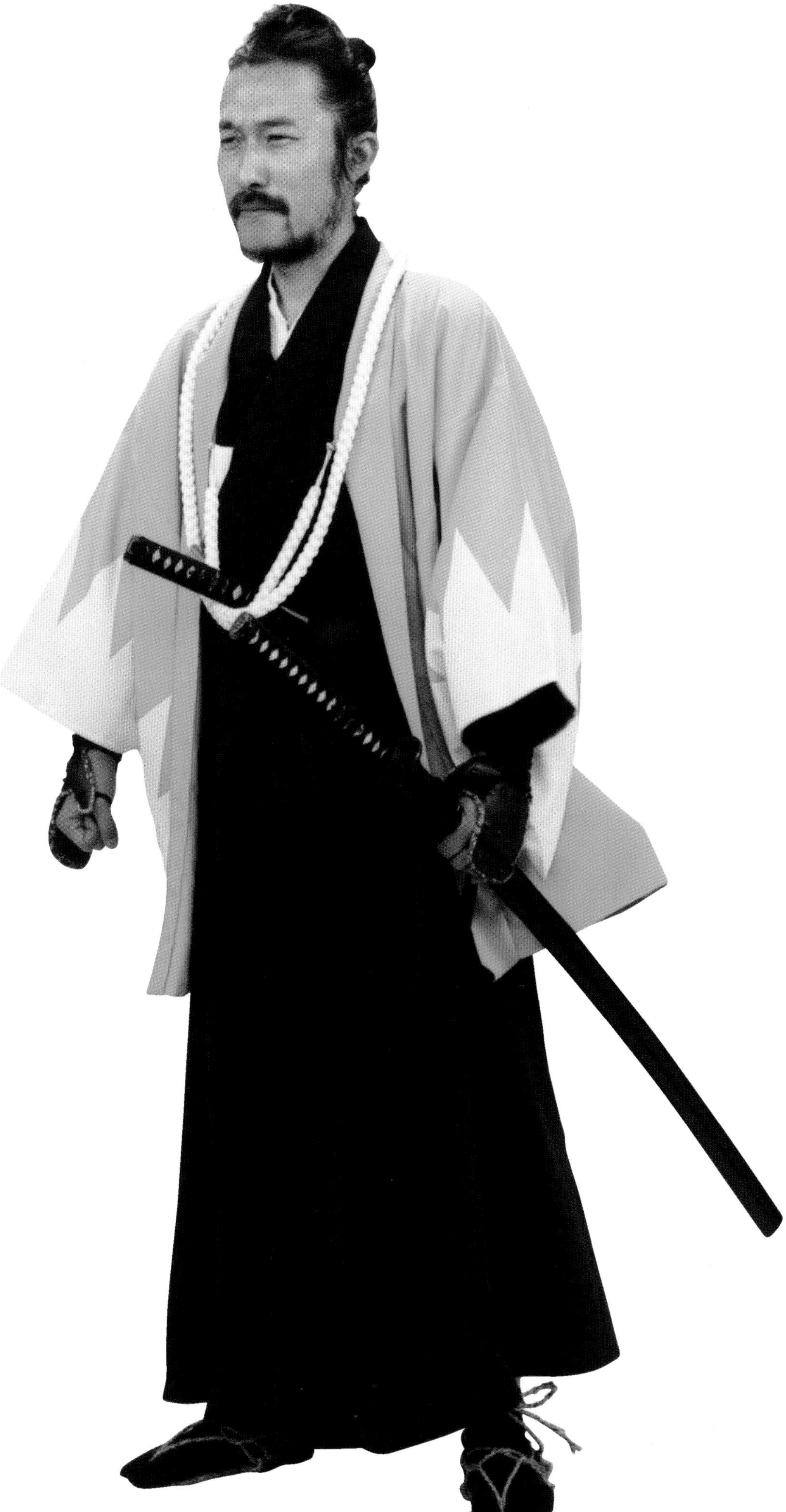

bakufu, which was eventually under command of Matsudaira Katamori in Aizuhan.

The swordsmen in the Shinsengumi consisted chiefly of lower-class samurai or non-samurai who, nevertheless, were proficient in the martial arts. They were recruited mainly from the suburbs of Edo city.

The Shinsengumi fought mercilessly against the outbreak of terror. Yet, things were soon to change and it was no so long before they themselves were perceived as being rebels.

This evolved for the initial class viewpoint in that they did not belonged to the true samurai class and were only later admitted as samurai. And while they served the samurai government to the very end, it was the daimyo warlords who mostly changed sides–as usual. So, who were the real rebels?

The Mimawarigumi differed from the Shinsengumi in that they were made up from the second or third sons of the Tokugawa bakufu old guard. They were also stationed in Kyoto, but their precise role and activities remain unclear.

However one thing known for certain is that they were engaged in Kyoto police duty. When they needed to raid an inn where anti-bakufu group were thought to be assembling, its members would needed some protection other than their sword, such as the wearing of arm protectors, gauntlets and carrying the jutte.

More sinisterly, such activities might also mean not hesitating to carry out assassin missions, muchin the same way as the enemy factions.

Right: *As seen from the rear, this member of the Shinsenguni is wearing his distinctive blue haori. The characterstic white cord of the outfit was tied here with its special knot, being a partial support for the policeman's dagger hilt at the front.*

Left: *This Mimawarigum swordsman is probably engaged in Kyoto police duty, as he is wearing kote forearm gauntlets and carries a jutte for arresting any wrongdoer.*

Right: *On legitimate special police duty; or perhaps engaged in a clandestine assasination attempt? The role and actions of the Mimawarigum were often of a dubious nature at this time.*

RONIN
Late Edo period

In the closing years of the Edo period, Japan became more and more open to foreign influences.

The Edo bakufu was rather slow, or maybe simply inefficient, in addressing this development, resulting in the frustrated opposition of the *ronin*, the low class samurai and youth who were very sensitive to and critical of the increased Western influence and the movement which supported the change.

Determined to resolve what they saw as a substantial problem and threat, and gathering their forces, they descended upon Kyoto. They became increasingly radical in their views and actions and dismissed any traditional way of pursuing their political views. Instead, they turned to direct action and assassination.

It was not only the bakufu samurai whom they attacked for resident foreigners also soon became their targets.

Unlike a previous disdain for such protection, the ronin's hat and straw rain cape and bamboo hat were distinctive items of dress, especially in wet weather

It was the actions and philosophy of the ronin and lower-class samurai that were fundamental in the basic drive to change Japanese society, albeit incorporating the swan song of the samurai as a class.

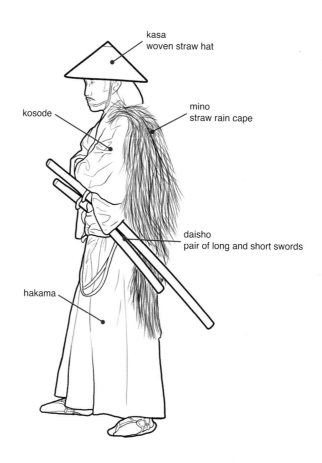

kasa
woven straw hat

kosode

mino
straw rain cape

daisho
pair of long and short swords

hakama

Right: *Without the hat and cape, does the ronin present a rather more sinister side as he belatedly turns to direct action against enemies and foreigners? Or is he simply kneeling in preparation for a council of war with a fellow samurai, as below?*

A ronin and samurai talking, seated in a way that is typical of the Edo period, but that is nowadays only adopted on formal occasions. Are they discussing their different ideologies? Or is the ronin trying to borrow some money from an official?

Above and right: *Ronin preparing for combat. The white cloth belt is typically that worn by the samurai when on the attack, as even the short-sleeved kosode was unsuitable when in action. This sway of wearing the belt was also adopted by women, but only for domestic duties such as room cleaning.*

CHRONOLOGY

All the following dates are given as conventional western AD style and convention.

As extensive chronologies of Japan's social, political and military history exist elsewhere, the dates below relate to the historical periods associated with the styles and changes in costume and dress as referred to in the descriptive texts.

Also included are dates of any events or that relate to specific persons who are also mentioned in the texts.

Early Japan
until 710

Early Heian Period
710-1150

794 Kanmu Emperor moves the court to Kyoto.

1035 Conflict between the warrior monks of Enjo and Enryaku temples.

1051 Start of the Zenkunen-no-eki "Nine Years War."

1056 Minamoto Yoriyoshi appointed *shogun*.

1129 Taira Tadamori suppresses pirates of the so-called Inland Sea.

Late Heian Period
1150-1192

1159 The Heishi acquire military supremacy.

Kamakura Period
1192-1333

1232 Regent Hojo Yasutoki proclaims the samurai code, gosei baishi kimoku.

1274 Mongol invasion repulsed.

1281 Second Mongol army invasion fails.

1333 Fall of the Kamakura bakufu.

1334 New imperial government established as Kenmu-no-shinsei.

1335 Ashikaga Takauji revolts against new government.

Muromachi Period
1336-1573

1336 The bakufu military government established in Kyoto. The era of Nanbokucho or the "Age of the Rival Courts" in Kyoto and Yoshino.

1338 Ashikaga Takauji appointed shogun.

1402 Relations established with the Ming Chinese emperor.

1457 Ota Dokan constructs the Edo Castle in Tokyo.

1467 Start of the Ohnin War in Kyoto.

1471 Opening of sanctuaries for the first Buddhist sects in Japan.

1477 End of the Ohnin War.

1543 The Portuguese introduce firearms to Japan.

1549 St. Francis Xavier's Christian mission to Nagasaki.

1560 Battle of Okehazama where Oda Nobunaga kills Imagawa Yoshimoto.

1572 Battle of Mikatagahara where Takeada Shingen defeats Tokugawa Ieyasu.

1576 Nobunaga starts the building of Azuchi Castle.

Senogoku Period
c.1450-early 1600s

The "Age of the Country at War" and a period of almost constant military conflict.

Azuichi-Momoyama Period
1573-1603

1582 Akechi Mitsuhide kills Oda Nobunaga at
   Honnoji temple.

1583 The rise of the warlord Toyotomi Hideyoshi
   and the war against Korea.

1590 Hideyoshi destroys the Hojo family and
   unites Japan.

1598 Death of Hideyoshi.

1600 Battle of Sekigahara where Tokugawa
   Ieyasu defeats Ishida Mitsunari and where
   the Ii family fought in their famed red armor.

Edo Period
1603-1868

1636 Death of the warlord Date Masamine,
   "One-eyed Jack."

1637 First Christian rebellion, in
   Shimabara.

1639 Bakufu prohibits visits by Portuguese
   ships.

1641 Bakufu transfers Dutch trading post to
   Dejima in Nagasaki.

1736 Russian ship appears in Chiba.

1793 Russian delegate arrives in Hokkaido.

1796 British ships visits Japan.

1801 Russian delegate visits Nagasaki to request
   trading rights.

1825 Bakufu orders foreign ships to be fired upon
   on sight.

1853 U.S. Navy under Commander Perry arrives at
   Hiraga.

1854 Treaty of Kanagawa.

1860 Commercial treaty signed with USA.

1863 Chochu Han fires on a British naval squadron
   off Shimonoseki.

1864 British, Dutch, French, and U.S. ships bombard
   Shimonoseki.

1867 Abdication of the shogun and restoration of
   imperial regime under the Meiji Emperor.

1868 Bakufu army defeated at Toba-Fushimi
   and the new government army defeats
   final rebels.

Meiji Period
1868-1912

1869 New government established in Edo, which is
   renamed Tokyo.

1877 Saigo Takamori dies as leader of the final,
   failed samurai rebellion in Kyushu.

Taisho and Early Showa Period
1912-1945

GLOSSARY

Many of the following terms are explained in the Introduction and subsequent main descriptions and are in *italics* at first reference there. Subsequent usage in the text is in normal type.

akuto Renegade or landless samurai, bandit or warrior monk of the late Kamakura-early Muromachi period.

anagamaki A variation of the *naginata* weapon.

ashigaru Light foot soldiers.

bakafu Literally the "tent government", because of a commander's tented field headquarters and then, by extension, the (effective) military) government of the shogun at the time.

bugyo Edo city magistrate.

daimon Style of *hitatare* that carried family crests or emblems.

daimyo High-class samurai warlord or feudal warrior baron.

doshin Edo city police inspector.

doubuku Jacket style of the Muromachi period.

ebira Arrow quiver.

eboshi Cap or soft hat.

gattari *Rear* fixing device on armor and for carrying a flag or similar device.

geta Wooden sandals.

gyoyo Apricot-leaf-shaped shoulder protector.

habaki Leg protectors.

hackimaki Headband style worn with an *eboshi*.

hakama General term for trousers and still in use.

haori Top layer armor of the Muromachi period.

hatspuri Face guard, sometimes called *happuri*.

hitatare Classic jacket-based costume.

hitoe Under-jacket.

hou Coat.

iai "Quick draw" sword deployment.

itsustuginu Early female garment, one of its several layers.

jinbaori Surcoat, often lavishly decorated and richly embroidered.

jingasa Edo city fire-fighter's helmet, usually worn with a cloth hood.

jobikeshi Edo city fire brigade.

junihitoe Ultimate stage of early female costume, literally "twelve layers in one".

jutte Literally "ten hands", Edo city police truncheon.

kabuki A traditional form of Japanese theater derived form the word for "unusual", etc. as below.

kabukikmono An "oddball" or eccentric dresser.

kaburaya Turnip-shaped arrow head.

kabuto Helmet protective flaps.

kami-shimo Literally "top and bottom", the full formal dress of the Edo period, with *katainu* and *hakama* of matching color and design.

kariginu Traditional hunting outfit.

katana Traditional samurai long sword worn blade uppermost.

katguinu Sleeveless *hitatre* jacket.

katsugi / katuga /kazuki Female *kimono* style as worn over the head.

kikutoji Decorative chrysanthemum-shaped knots or seam reinforcements.

kimono Generic name for traditional Japanese clothing, but usually female in modern usage.

kogusoko Type of light armor.

kosode Shirt-like jacket, literally "small/short sleeves".

kote Upper body armor.

kusazuri Thigh armor.

mino Straw raincoat.

mo Lady's skirt-like garment.

motodori Traditional samurai tied hair-knot.

naginata Classic samurai pole-mounted, bladed weapon.

nanbanjin Literally "southern barbarian" but used generically at the time to describe virtually all non-Japanese.

noh Traditional religious dance that is now a classical Japanese theatrical form.

obi Belt or sash.

ohguchi Underwear shorts tied at the side.

okubyo-ita Back armor protection, the so-called "coward's board".

okikukuri Young man's sleeve decoration.

oyoroi Type of light armor.

ronin Land-less and master-less rebel samurai of the late nineteenth century.

shikami Mythical horned beast, often used as a helmet embellishment.

shirokosode General term for underwear.

shogun Originally, a temporary rank bestowed upon an expeditionary commander-in-chief, but later the title or rank of the military dictator governing in parallel to the Emperor's court.

sode Shoulder guard or protection.

suikan Ornate jacket of the Kamakura period.

suoho Traditional jacket.

tabi Sock-like footwear.

tachi Traditional samurai long sword worn blade downwards.

tarikubi Folded-down neck style of the *suikan*.

tentsuki Helmet decorative device.

teppo Samurai (chiefly arquebus) gunner.

uchigatna Later development of the *tachi* sword.

uchikake Female coat-like garment.

uenohakama Under-trousers.

ukiorimono Style of splendid silk embroidery on a lady's *kimono*.

utigi Cape-like female jacket or short coat, sometimes alsocalled an *utiki*.

utsobo Box-like type of arrow quiver.

watagami Shoulder straps.

yari Spear

yofuku Japanese term for any type of western style dress.

yoriki Edo city police chief inspector.

zhori Type of sandal.

zunari (kabuo) Type of "head-shaped" helmet.

INDEX

This index is of a general nature, as the book also contains a Glossary and Chronology (see previous pages). There is also an extensive Introduction, in which the origins and developments of samurai armor and associated costume are described.

The book's coverage of historical and cultural periods can be found in the Contents